TUNING
INTO MOM

"*Tuning into Mom* lives up to its title's promise by helping readers understand the mind-set of moms. The authors "listened" to over 4,500 moms, capturing invaluable insights for businesses, marketers, and researchers across a range of consumer categories.

As a marketer to moms, it is critical to understand mom's values and attitudes. I can complement that understanding with the rich insights in this book. I know you'll find it just as valuable for your business, whether it's technology or textiles."

~ *Brigette Wolf, Brand Manager, Global Oreo Innovation, Kraft Foods*

"With more than twenty-five years of experience leading consumer-driven businesses and brands in categories ranging from restaurants to wireless, I know how important it is to capture the hearts and minds of moms. *Tuning into Mom* provides a fresh perspective for brands that recognize mom as an important purchaser or purchase influencer of their goods and services. It will certainly stimulate new thinking and generate category-specific creative solutions to better impact mom as a consumer and influencer. It's an important read for marketers in any industry."

~ *Mary N. Dillon, President and CEO, U.S. Cellular*

A very pragmatic and balanced blend of consumer and brand insights coupled with the appropriate amount of data. It covers the spectrum of "Mom for all Ages."

~ *Jean-Marie Dolenc, General Manager, Hospital Pharmaceutical International Marketing, Abbott Labs*

"As a marketing executive who is challenged with finding pragmatic actions in a highly competitive market, I value resources that provide deep, foundational insights. With *Tuning into Mom*, Michal Clements and Teri Lucie Thompson have delivered—pun intended—such a resource, a first-born winner. The book proves a unique hypothesis about children's influence on moms' buying behavior, and at the same time, reinforces to all marketers the importance of targeting mom, the household CFO and chief buyer."

~ *Pam El, Marketing Vice President, State Farm Insurance*

"Whether you're a marketer, at an agency, or simply interested in understanding the most powerful force in the marketplace, *Tuning into Mom* by Michal Clements and Teri Lucie Thompson give us a game-changing insight that will unlock the potential for brands and businesses for years to come. With fresh data and a savvy-smart approach, this book is a how-to manual for creating demand today. But more than that, Michal and Teri show us that when we understand mom, and create products and services that meet her specific needs, we're not only making the world better for her, but for all those children and families she influences."

~*Dave Kissell, President and CEO, InStadium*

"Rich insights, clever case studies, a fine blend of data and real customer stories . . . What more could a marketer want? Fresh ideas on marketing to moms based on the age of their children? Check! *Tuning into Mom* delivers all this and more. Kudos to first-time authors Michal Clements and Teri Lucie Thompson who really did their homework and have added to the slow-growing body of knowledge around marketing to moms. Studying and writing about gender-specific marketing for over twenty years, I gained new insights in reading this book. You will too!"

> ~ *Marti Barletta, author of* Marketing to Women, PrimeTime Women, *and* Trends: Recognize, Analyze, Capitalize

"*Tuning into Mom* is a timely field guide for marketing-driven organizations looking to target mothers. The Theme Resource Guides provide laser focus to unique mom segments and their priorities relative to products, and the case studies beautifully illustrate how solid strategy and marketing creativity come together."

> ~ *Sarah Merz, CEO, FranklinCovey Products*

"*Tuning into Mom* provides deep insight into the things that moms care about most for children of different ages, as well as for themselves. Moms are making or influencing decisions for their children well into adulthood. Marketers should leverage the practical framework in this book to position their products and services in the most relevant way to this powerful target audience."

> ~ *Karen R. Haefling, Chief Marketing and Communications Officer, KeyCorp*

"Brilliant. Methodical. Right on time. *Tuning into Mom* draws on a robust body of comprehensive research and a never-ending stream of marketing insights to provide an extraordinary view into the rich and diverse landscape of moms in America. Michal Clements and Teri Lucie Thompson profoundly illuminate the most effective ways for brands to reach moms with relevant solutions and authentic messaging. I highly recommend this path-breaking volume to any marketer that is committed to taking a genuine brand leadership position within this powerful segment."

> ~ *Eddie R. Navarrete, Marketing Director, T-Mobile USA*

"One of the most important axioms in marketing is to 'control the pathways.' It is the marketers' imperative to understand who influences one's customers and make sure you are communicating to and targeting them as well. *Tuning into Mom* does an excellent job of explaining the roles mothers play in the decisions of their families. The book will not only allow the reader to understand this important market segment, but will also challenge the reader to better understand how they can win in the marketplace by "helping moms help their families." I highly recommend this book for college courses as well! It is in the same league as classics like *Why We Buy*."

> ~ *Tom Hayes, Ph.D., Professor of Marketing, Xavier University*

"*Tuning into Mom* provides fresh insight into the ongoing influence of moms on young adults. From my experience, I also know that many moms are interested in promoting wholesome eating for their children. For a casual dining chain, this spells opportunity. *Tuning into Mom* is a must-read for agencies and clients that are looking for fresh thinking and new ideas on how to capture the spending of mom, as well as her young adult child."

> ~ *Mark Gilley, Vice President, Consumer Insights, Darden Restaurants*

"As a beauty writer and mother myself, I find the authors' insights into marketing to moms in both the real and virtual worlds right on target. Their book, *Tuning into Mom*, offers great perspective on how and where mothers shop for beauty and fashion and how their buying habits, priorities, and sense of personal style shift as their children grow and they move through different stages of motherhood."

> ~ *Andrea Pomerantz Lustig, author of* How to Look Expensive *and contributing beauty editor of* Glamour Magazine

"Marketing and brand building can only be successful with deep understanding of the target audience. Teri Lucie Thompson and Michal Clements have done a spectacular job of peeling back the layers of the critical target audience—moms—and providing the insights needed to effectively reach them. A must-read for any marketer with moms on their mind, *Tuning into Mom* is the engaging and enlightening book that will open your eyes to the mom possibilities for your brand."

> ~ Donna Heckler, co-author of *The Truth About Creating Brands People Love,* Brand Strategy Lead, Ingersol-Rand

TUNING
INTO MOM

UNDERSTANDING AMERICA'S MOST POWERFUL CONSUMER

MICHAL CLEMENTS TERI LUCIE THOMPSON

PURDUE UNIVERSITY PRESS | WEST LAFAYETTE, INDIANA

Library of Congress Cataloging-in-Publication Data

Clements, Michal, 1963-

  Tuning into mom : understanding America's most powerful consumer / Michal Clements and Teri Lucie Thompson.

     p. cm.

  Includes bibliographical references and index.

  ISBN 978-1-55753-585-6 (cloth) -- ISBN 978-1-61249-170-7 (epdf) -- ISBN 978-1-61249-171-4 (epub) 1. Mothers--United States--Attitudes. 2. Consumer behavior--United States. 3. Consumers' preferences--United States. 4. Relationship marketing--United States. I. Thompson, Teri Lucie, 1956- II. Title.

  HQ759.C54 2011

  306.874'3--dc23

                              2011023368

CONTENTS

ACKNOWLEDGMENTS

In no particular order, we would like to thank:

Our partners in the Marketing to Moms Coalition. Accomplished marketers, businesswomen, and authors, these amazing colleagues help us stretch our thinking, expand our network, and find solutions. Generous with their information, time, goodwill, and vision, their friendship and knowledge has made us better marketers and better storytellers. Our kudos and appreciation to Bridget Brennan, Amy Colton, and Maria Bailey.

Marti Barletta. Not only because she helped define and crystallize a new body of knowledge in the women's marketing space, but also because of her generous soul. Marti helped us refine our hypothesis and generously shared her experiences as an author.

Our research subjects. We cannot thank them all by name, but we do want to acknowledge our first three interviewees, who were invaluable in helping us launch the qualitative phase of our project. First, Melanie Holtan, now a State Farm agency executive, and a mother of two with a knack for describing what many moms are experiencing. Her keen insight, quick wit, and quotable observations felt like a buoy in the rough waters of ambiguity when we started this project. Second, we thank Carla Lucie for "taking one for the family" and sharing candid insights about the teenage years. Finally, we appreciate Sally Kahle's ability to toggle between toddler and teenage years. As her child aged, she provided us with insight about how drivers of moms' decision making change over time.

Insight to Action consulting staff. Their help was invaluable. In particular, Maria Gracia, Ketul Patel, Laura Ehlers, Ashleigh Meyn, Elise Baskel, Marcy Blight, Marcia Delaney, Samantha Holland, Chuck Greenia, and the ever-helpful Trudy Delfosse.

Insight to Action Advisory Board members. A special thanks to the Insight to Action Advisory Board members who provided ongoing counsel, wisdom, and support: George Chivari, Larry Burns, Leslie Berger, Judy Harrison, and Bram Bluestein.

DDB Chicago and Tribal DDB—especially Dave Schneider, Kathleen O'Hara, Shawn Powers, and Debbie McKean, who were instrumental in creating and pitching the red portfolio concept to Teri during her time at State Farm. Although they are no longer at DDB, we have a soft spot in our hearts for them and for the agency.

State Farm—especially Jack Weekes, Pam El, and Leif Roll, who serendipitously introduced the two of us. They have always encouraged new thinking and focus on customer segments. Also, we appreciate the company for its ongoing work in customer segment marketing, as well as for creating a new role for Teri and giving her the resources to explore and succeed.

Walmart and Current Lifestyle Marketing/Weber Shandwick. Generous underwriters of the *State of the American Mom* research and thought partners on the most pertinent issues for moms, especially Ramon Portilla and Amy Colton.

Our endorsers. Thanks for reading chapters in their unedited state, for your belief in us, and for your kind words of support.

Carol Rest. Graphic designer extraordinaire, Carol beautifully translated our content into cover art that complements the title. We appreciate her nod to our love of shopping!

Linda Terhune. An excellent writer in her own right, Linda helped us find our way through a couple of sticky chapters by asking good questions and ghostwriting a few paragraphs.

Our families:

- **Lyle Thompson.** Your patience, belief, support, and love are always a blessing, but were especially invaluable throughout this project. Thank you for asking great questions, sharing your opinions on everything from cover art to pseudonyms, and for your generous supply of hugs along the way.

- **Dick and Nancy Lucie.** Thank you never seems like enough to say to the world's best parents; insufficient as it is, thank you for instilling in me the belief that "where there's a will, there's a way," the work ethic to finish what I start, and the intellectual curiosity to tackle projects like this.

- **Cliff Porzenheim.** Thank you for encouraging my latest venture, in this case writing a book. Additionally, I appreciate your support of my other extracurriculars, like starting a company (twice) and planning overly extravagant birthday parties.

- **Christopher Porzenheim.** Thank you for your immediate grasp of the big idea and talent for boil-down thinking; your strong emphasis that we focus more on the Theme Resource Guide and the age and theme matrix; and your patience, interest in, and passion for the work.

- **M J Porzenheim.** You always challenge your mom to take risks, including parasailing, roller coasters, foreign travel, and other ventures. You are a delightful, stimulating friend.

You! Thank you for your interest in this work and for the work you have done or will do to "tune into mom"!

PREFACE

To help you grasp the content of the following chapters, we want to share how this book came to be—the inspiration for the work, some context on what makes it unique, and an overview of our research and writing journey.

In the beginning (or, more accurately, in 2004), Teri worked for State Farm Insurance in its corporate marketing department, and she assumed responsibility for the company's customer segment marketing division. The company had recently transitioned from a property/casualty and life insurer to a full-fledged financial services company, offering bank and securities products in addition to insurance. It needed to refresh its customer insights to effectively market its full suite of products to customers.

Inspired by Marti Barletta's book *Marketing to Women* (Dearborn 2003) and working with Michal in her role as owner and principal of Insight to Action, a firm focused on building brands through discoveries that result in specific business-building actions, Teri led a team that developed a body of insights to help the company more effectively target women—with specific emphasis on moms and small business owners. One key determination— that women desire more context and information prior to making financial services decisions—led to the creation of State Farm's "red portfolio" motif and micro site (www.sfredportfolio.com). As its popularity and success grew, so did Teri's opportunities to address external audiences. During one of her presentations to a New York City advertising group, she met fellow presenter Maria Bailey, author of *Trillion-Dollar Moms, Marketing to Moms, Mom 3.0*, and *The Ultimate Mom*. Energized by Maria's shared passion, Teri wondered how to pull together resources around marketing to women, particularly mothers, for the benefit of others without sacrificing proprietary knowledge.

She approached Maria about establishing a nonprofit coalition that could function as a repository of information for marketers like herself who were trying to serve a demographic untapped for too long. With Maria's interest, the Marketing to Moms Coalition began its gestation period. A few months later, with the addition of Bridget Brennan, CEO of Female Factor and author of *Why She Buys* (formerly of Zeno's Speaking Female division); Amy Colton, EVP at Current Lifestyle Marketing (also formerly at Zeno); and Michal, the Marketing to Moms Coalition became a reality.

At the same time, Teri pondered ongoing challenges in the women's marketing segment. She was particularly intrigued about how women, and moms specifically, made decisions in a variety of categories, and she wondered specifically about women's decision making in the financial services category, which was the focus of her employment. Writers like Marti Barletta, Maria Bailey, and Mary Lou Quinlan had laid a great foundation, raising the corporate consciousness around gender-specific marketing. She envisioned stories told by women specific to various topics and categories in which moms have high interest—for example, food, technology, and clothing. These stories, including case examples of successful brands that captured the attention of moms in these areas, would add color to the personal insights unique to each category. The stories would bring the moms' needs to life, while data would illustrate the trends. After plotting for a few months, she realized one of her favorite thinking partners could help, so she approached Michal about partnering on a project.

Thus began this journey. At that point in time, *Tuning into Mom* was a concept for a book in search of the detailed research and specific insights to make it concrete, and the words to bring it to you.

In the early phases of the work, we conducted in-depth interviews to identify initial "hot buttons," themes and brands that moms felt did a good job in addressing their concerns. We were excited to discover the rich interaction between moms of teenagers and young adults, and how these moms continue to influence their children's brand decisions and choices. We also saw how these moms held themselves to a high standard, often conducting considerable research for greater context in order to provide their child with the best possible input. This was another manifestation of the earlier insight, and now it was applied in additional areas. For example, a mom might conduct the legwork for her teenager in identifying some appropriate colleges to consider. Even more interesting is that we found teenagers welcomed their moms' research in many cases as they saw that their mom had their best interests at heart. Later on in the interviews we honed in specifically on the areas of greatest interest by age of child. Another discovery along the way was the quantitative finding that the most helpful lens to understand mom was by understanding the age of her oldest child living at home. This key insight was uncovered by Insight to Action consultants while conducting *State of the American Mom* (*SOAM*) analysis. After the research and writing of the book was complete, Michal joined The Cambridge Group, where she has the privilege to work with colleagues who share her passion for go-to-market action strategies based on robust customer and consumer insights.

Another important element in this narrative is the (*SOAM*) survey. When we began the Marketing to Moms Coalition, our work focused on aggregating existing information about successful practices in marketing to moms, as well as recognizing companies that did this well. (The HER Award is given annually by the Coalition to a company that creates high-impact marketing campaigns that **h**onor, **e**mpower, and **r**espect mothers; see more at http://marketingtomoms.org/herAwards/index.php.) The need for benchmarking and ongoing tracking of moms' attitudes and purchasing behavior, as well as actionable data and insights on American moms for retailers, manufacturers, and other professionals who market to them, quickly became apparent to the group. Thus, in 2007, we created the first (*SOAM*) survey, which has been executed annually since then. This survey provides a rich data source for analyzing moms' attitudes and behaviors. It is also important to note that all five members of the Coalition provided input on the survey, which was designed, fielded, and analyzed by Insight to Action.

We have included some of this analysis in the book, using it to illustrate purchase patterns. We trust you will find this analysis—as well as the detailed case studies—particularly interesting, as this material is often contained only in internal company analyses. In fact, the type of detailed quantitative information found in the *SOAM* report is often commissioned by companies and not available to the general public. The insights about moms are used to develop growth strategies and actions to build brands in a wide range of categories from automotive, to clothing and shoes, to cruise lines, to financial services, to restaurants and packaged goods. We hope you see this as one of the benefits of this book—an "inside baseball" look at original research that would usually be very expensive or impossible to access.

Speaking of you, we do not know who you are, but we are glad you have joined us. We think this work will be particularly useful to marketers, manufacturers of consumer goods, and services geared toward mothers and their children (of any age from to infant/toddler to young adult), as well as academics teaching consumer behavior or marketing strategy courses. We trust you will find these insights useful and hope you will pass this along to friends and acquaintances—especially those who fall into these categories.

CHAPTER 1

Tuning Into Mom: Her Priorities and Hot Buttons

Why is Mom So Important to Marketers?

Mom is a popular topic these days. A quick search of Amazon reveals over twenty-two thousand books on the subject of mom, ranging from historical reviews (*Mom: The Transformation of Motherhood in Modern America.*) to appreciation (*Why a Daughter Needs a Mom*) to self-help (*Mojo Mom: Nurturing Your Self While Raising a Family* or *Sippy Cups Are Not for Chardonnay: And Other Things I Had to Learn as a New Mom*). The experience of motherhood is a defining feature of our society, and "mom" is an important social and cultural identifier.

Clearly, with over seventy-seven million moms in the United States, these household CFOs are also an important customer group—in charge of spending an estimated $2.4 trillion collectively in the United States.[1] However, mom's spending influence is much greater than this $2.4 trillion she directly controls, because she also influences the current and future purchases of her older children in an array of categories such as consumer products, financial services, and travel. And the future mom market will remain sizable over the foreseeable future, with over 4.25 million births recorded in 2008.[2]

Simply put, improvements in attracting and retaining moms as customers, as purchase influencers of their children, and as referred providers of other moms will yield rich returns. While many brand leaders are defining moms as an important customer group, too often we find that these brands work with broad definitions such as "women ages twenty-five to forty-nine with children under eighteen living at home." These overly broad, monolithic target definitions do not provide the rich insight needed to effectively develop strategies and actions to reach mom. They fail to recognize the significant changes in the mom's focus and needs based on the age of her child. Finding better ways to understand the mom market is the focus of this book.

Digging into the Data

The broad age of child segments that we will explore in this book are the following: moms of infants/toddlers (children under age two), moms of preschoolers (children ages three to six), moms of elementary school kids (children ages seven to nine), moms of middle schoolers (children ages ten to twelve), moms of teenagers (children ages thirteen to seventeen), and moms of young adults (children ages eighteen to twenty-nine). We explain further in the Appendix how we came to select these age ranges and give details of the methodologies we used to understand the different behaviors of these groups.

To build a deeper understanding of American moms, this book uses four data sources: (1) a range of primary and secondary research, including a robust, quantitative fact base with the responses of over four thousand moms; (2) over twenty in-depth personal interviews; (3) a due-diligence review of existing research; and (4) brand case study research.

Quantitatively, the Marketing to Moms Coalition's report, the *State of the American Mom* (*SOAM*), contains a wealth of information providing extensive insight into emerging trends within different groups of moms. Since 2007, the research has been conducted by the Marketing to Moms Coalition as part of its commitment to furthering the understanding of America's most powerful consumers through research. Each year, the Coalition uses a panel provider to contact a nationally representative sample of American moms via online invitation. As part of this research, Insight to Action compares over thirty different subgroups for the Marketing to Moms Coalition, (e.g., moms by age of child, income, ethnicity, etc.). In 2009 and 2010, the cost of this research was underwritten by Weber Shandwick and Current Lifestyle Marketing. In 2008, 2009, and 2010, with support from Walmart, the survey also included a sample of two hundred Spanish-speaking moms to be analyzed as a separate group.

The quantitative approach not only allows for the identification of overarching trends, but also can yield more refined insights into the specific groups of moms who are driving those trends and behaviors.

The *SOAM* research explores a wide range of topics, such as mom's top priorities; family economics; environmental engagement; shopping tendencies; child influence in purchase decisions, food, and nutrition; and media habits and preferences. For our purposes, most of the information from the research that is covered in this book focuses on responses to the priority themes of moms by age of child, particularly the oldest child. Of note, there are many other interesting topics contained in the research that we do not address given the book's focus. For more information on this research, please consult the Appendix.

Additionally, we conducted over twenty in-depth interviews among moms of children ages one to twenty-nine. Participants were recruited via a large network of family and friends and were rigorously managed to be balanced on age of child(ren), household size, income, and ethnicity. Of note, child age groups are not mutually exclusive; some of the moms we interviewed had more than one child living at home and therefore were asked to share their perspectives and concerns on each child separately. In keeping with our practice, we asked them to focus first on their oldest child, and then compare and contrast with younger siblings.

Two phases of qualitative interviews were completed. The first phase had a broader scope and helped to identify and refine the hot-button themes. The second phase of interviews was completed after the themes had been identified, and as a result, generally focused on the theme areas. In both phases moms were encouraged to add any additional priorities or perspective. Moms were asked to describe their experiences and candidly share their opinions on key topics explored in this book, as well as any related concerns. These "mommy mind" narratives are included throughout this text for a more fully dimensioned look into their emotions, needs, and decision-making processes.

The third resource was a due-diligence review of existing research including journals, similar studies, government data, and corporate publications to supplement our findings and/or provide a different perspective. We also conducted Internet research to obtain moms' opinions from blog and forum posts.

Case study brands were identified by moms in the qualitative interviews, as well as through suggestions from branding experts and our own experience. The case studies were developed using published sources, including articles and news releases from third parties, as well as through interviewing select brand leaders for case study products that target moms. Each chapter also includes two or more specific brand case histories with related marketing approaches highlighted to demonstrate how organizations have addressed moms' needs by leveraging age of child and topical insights. We have aligned the case studies by age of child. As an example, the Apple iPhone is a brand that has developed specific, successful branding efforts for moms of toddlers. Functionally, the Apple iPhone provides a toddler mom with a multipurpose phone, Internet access, GPS, camera, and camcorder device all in one. Perhaps even more interestingly, the iPhone can provide mom with a break by entertaining her child. This toddler-friendly technology truly brings the term "easy to use" to a new level and addresses a market segment (toddlers) that most other phone and PDA brands had overlooked.

How to Use This Book

What are "Hot-Button" Topic Areas/Themes?

"Hot-button" areas are topical and/or purchase areas in which mom is particularly sensitized. There is a well-known maxim that the best way to quickly get a woman's attention (if she has children, including adult children) is to talk with her and engage her in a dialog about her children. Mom will be even more engaged if the communication also addresses the theme areas she cares about most. Aligning one's communication approach to these hot-button areas will communicate with mom emotionally and powerfully.

This approach to targeting mom's concerns to capture her communication interest is relevant for the spending that she directly controls, and also for her children's considerable spending, which mom influences.

In this book we examine mom's overall priority hot-button areas, which are shared by moms at a high level across children's ages. As a starting point, addressing these hot-button themes will pique mom's interest, so that she is receptive to the brand's message. However, the approach must be taken a step further to consider the theme in light of the age of her oldest child to be most effective and relevant.

The major hot-button areas that we will explore in this book (and that hold the greatest interest) are the following:

1. Food

2. Exercise and Sports

3. Education

4. Safety and Health

5. Technology

6. Fashion and Beauty

These topical focus areas emerged through our qualitative interviews with moms on an open-ended basis and through the Coalition's quantitative *SOAM* research.

The book follows a structured approach with individual chapters that examine each of the six hot-button areas through the lens of the six age-of-child segments (i.e., infant/toddler, preschooler, elementary schoolchild, middle schooler, teenager, and young adult). This allows the reader to readily locate the information that is most applicable to his or her organization, depending on the age of child and the hot-button topic of interest.

Each chapter also includes two or more specific brand case histories with related marketing approaches highlighted to demonstrate how organizations have addressed moms' needs by leveraging age of child and topical insights. We have aligned the case studies by age of child.

What are "Theme Resource Guides"?

Each chapter includes a summary chart, called a "Theme Resource Guide." The light, medium, and dark grays identify mom's concerns ("hot-button" themes) by priority level to mom (low, medium, high) and by the age of her child. Each guide includes content relevant to the child ("Mom's Concern for Her Child" version), and content relevant to the mom ("Mom's Concern for Herself" version).

An example of the Theme Resource Guide—the "Mom's Concern for Her Child" version—is shown on the next page.

While subsequent chapters will examine each major hot-button theme in greater depth, we are introducing this tool at the outset to aid the reader in navigating the book to find the areas of greatest relevance. To use the guide, the reader can first select a theme or themes of greatest interest. For example, consider that the topic of food is selected. Then the reader can scan down the column for food to identify the overall priority of the food "hot button" by age of child. The shading indicates the priority, and generally we can see that food is a moderate to high priority for moms with children in

Mom's Concern for Her Child

THEME RESOURCE GUIDE

	Food	Exercise and Sports	Education	Safety and Health	Technology	Fashion and Beauty
Infant/Toddler Moms	• Good overall nutrition and developing broad taste palate	• Sports not a focus • Exercise by moving around	• Gross motor skills and cognitive stimulation	• Physical safety • Adult supervision	• Entertainment (e.g., iPhone)	• Comfort/move freely • Some individuality
Preschool Moms	• "Healthy," fruits and vegetables, avoid excess sugar	• Keeping kid active • Sports starting	• Gross motor skills and cognitive stimulation • Socialization • Pre-K skills—colors, shapes	• Physical safety • Adult supervision	• Entertainment • Education	• Comfort/move freely • Some individuality
Elementary School Moms	• "Healthy," fruits and vegetables • Fuel for the day	• Sports participation family lifestyle	• Adjustment to classroom • Academic building blocks	• Playground/sports safety • Stranger danger	• Entertainment • Education	• Presentable for school • Sports affiliation
Middle School Moms	• Dinner focus • Encourage healthy choices	• Sports focus	• Academic foundation • Getting good grades	• Cyber safety • Sports safety	• Entertainment • Check in with mom	• Emerging adult image—appropriate look
Moms of Teens	• Encourage healthy on-the-go choices	• Depends on whether child plays sports	• Grade • College Scholarship	• Teen driving, drinking, drugs, sex ed	• Check in with mom • Entertainment	• Veto power—too low-cut
Moms of Young Adults	• Recipe and cooking advice • Guidance on better choices	• More concerns with adult child's exercise but little ability to impact	• Career/job results from education • Making good choices	• Some concerns around driving • Health insurance coverage	• Lifeline between parent and child	• Coach child to dress as adult/project right image in key situations (e.g., job interview)

■ = Higher Mom's priority
■ = Moderate Mom's priority
□ = Lower Mom's priority

the age ranges from infant/toddler to middle schooler. We can see that this topic is relatively less important for moms of teenagers and young adults.

The next step for the reader is to examine the text in the individual cells of the grid as this wording provides more specificity on mom's focus at that age range. For example, moms of young adults will provide recipes and cooking advice as well as counsel on better food choices when asked by their adult children. In comparison, the mom of an elementary schoolchild has greater focus on making sure her child eats enough nutritious foods, including fruits and vegetables, so that the child can perform in his or her busy day of school and extracurriculars.

The reader can then consider whether and how to align the corporate brand using these insights. For example, a brand could sponsor an adult child and mom cooking contest with a cook-off event. The brand does not have to be a food product; for instance, it could be a communications services provider that is celebrating the importance of food (along with communications) in forging family ties and passing along both new and old traditions. A slightly different twist could be for the young adult to introduce the mom to a new recipe.

Insights to Action

During our research, several patterns emerged that permeate the rest of the book that we believe are of great practical importance to executives who manage brands as they proceed to implementation. We refer to these as "Insights to Action."

Moms of Older Children Matter

In considering branding initiatives that overtly target moms, our observation is that many of the "mom-focused" marketing messages address mainly moms in the youngest child age ranges, specifically infants, toddlers, and preschoolers. While moms of elementary schoolchildren also receive focus, branding efforts are greatly reduced for moms whose children are middle school age or older. We appreciate the strategy of a brand choosing to focus on only the older teenager or young adult, but our research reveals that, at times, this approach stems from an old paradigm that does not accurately reflect the frequent consultation and communication between today's older children and their moms. Our research finds that for certain topics, mom's influence remains strong even in the young adult years of eighteen to twenty-nine, and that today's young adults are in frequent contact with their moms on a wide range of topics.

Consider that of seventy-seven million moms in the United States, only nine million have children in the infant and toddler range, while approximately ten million have children in the preschool range (ages three to five). However, there are more than twenty-five million moms of young adults (ages eighteen to twenty-nine) and another twelve million of teenagers (ages fourteen to seventeen).[3]

We observe that mom's influence in decision making with middle schoolers, teenagers, young adults, and even older adult children is a missed opportunity for brands. In many cases, mom is easier to reach than the child, and she continues to either make the decision outright and/or significantly influence her offspring.

Mom's influence on her older child's spending is seen in two ways. The first way is through brand preferences and habits developed during childhood and/or adolescence (for example, "I use that brand because it's the one I grew up with and my mother purchased" or "I considered going to that college because mom took me there for her college reunions so I felt comfortable"). The second way is through consultation. We find that today's young adults frequently consult with their mothers as a trusted resource on categories with which they are less familiar. For example, they will ask their parents for advice on insurance or work and career decisions.

The Oldest Child Has the Most Impact

We examined the information on the age of child through multiple lenses to determine which approach yielded more distinct insights. Specifically, we looked at families that included any child in the age segment, those that included only one child in the age segment, and those with the oldest child in the age segment. For purposes of the greatest insight on marketplace demand, we found that honing the mom's focus on the oldest child in the age segment was more impactful than the other alternatives. So, while age of the child living at home is the most important factor overall, we have also learned that it can be helpful to develop branding programs and product offerings by focusing mom specifically on her oldest child at home, instead of asking her to consider all children simultaneously, or asking her to focus primarily on the younger children in her family.

Our experience is that mom typically puts disproportionate focus on her answers for her oldest child. In a sense, her attention is taken up more by this child as they go through each experience for the first time together. This is, of course, barring exceptional circumstances such as children with special needs or significant gaps in the children's birth years. As almost every parent will recognize, mom typically takes many times more pictures of her first child than she does of subsequent children, documenting each milestone. Related to this greater amount of attention focused on the oldest child, we also observe that the greatest need is found in first-time moms connecting to and being affirmed by other moms with a child of a similar age. First-time moms are, as the name suggests, moms who have never had a child living at home previously, and so they are experiencing the parental journey for the "first time." Before social networking tools existed, and persisting since their inception, moms found other moms to connect with in hospital prenatal classes, neighborhood sandboxes and play lots, and through secular and religious community groups. With the explosion of the Internet and social media, it is even easier for moms to locate other women with children of similar age. It is also even easier for moms to influence the purchasing decisions of other women who are in similar circumstances (e.g., through online recommendations).

The result is that we find that the more discriminating results come from focusing the mom on her oldest child. However, this is not meant to imply that these moms are the sole target audience, rather that they yield the greatest insights.

Hot-Button Areas Morph

We see the focus of hot-button areas morph over time. Consider safety. While the safety of her child is critically important to all moms, the focus changes as the child ages. For example, cyber safety and concerns with cyberbullying and stalking take on much more relevance to mom when her child reaches the middle school years. Additionally, the physical safety risks to which an infant is most vulnerable differ dramatically from the physical safety issues of a teenager, with teen driving a particularly sensitive area for moms of teens.

Bringing It All Together

Seventy-seven million moms of children ages twenty-nine or younger directly control $2.4 trillion in spending and influence even more than that when their children's purchases are taken into account. The age of child is a critical determining factor in mom's thought process and filters her decision making. Major hot-button areas and themes are attention hooks that organizations can use to emotionally connect with moms, tailored for relevancy by age of child.

These findings are built on a robust foundation of primary and secondary research, a due-diligence review of the literature, and case studies of brands that have addressed moms' priorities.

Understanding the hot-button themes by age of child is a critical framework for organizations that recognize moms as an important customer to understand. The brand or organization can select the specific age and theme insight to use to create its strategy, and also to develop products or services that address mom's priorities. The brand can also use the relevant theme insight to develop communications that will be embraced by moms, or to select sponsorships that align the brand to mom's priorities.

Importantly, we have found that the age of child answer can be further refined to take into account an important consideration: how does or how can a brand align with a hot-button priority and concern area for moms? Developing your brand's marketing efforts using the segmented age and hot-button theme approach will meaningfully improve your brand's chance of getting mom's attention and of building connections with her.

So, let's start "tuning into Mom."

Notes

1. Maria T. Bailey, *Power Moms: The New Rules for Engaging Mom Influencers Who Drive Brand Choice,* Wyatt-MacKenzie Publishing, Inc., 2011, 13.
2. Laura B. Shrestha and Elayne J. Heisler, "The Changing Demographic Profile of the United States," accessed March 11, 2011, http://www.fas.org/sgp/crs/misc/RL32701.pdf.
3. Bureau of the Census (November 2009 and November 1999), Current Population Survey for Moms and analysis by Insight to Action, Inc. for Young Adults (January 2010).

CHAPTER 2

Food: Stealth Veggies and Panini Making

The topic of food and nutrition is a critical, complex, and, at times, contradictory hot-button area for moms. For a mom, feeding her child is so central to her role that the topic commands a considerable portion of her attention and time. Arguably, one part of the unstated definition of a "good" mother is one who feeds and cares for her child well so that the child thrives. In many cultures, a plump baby is seen as a sign of health and good parenting. Starting even before the child is born, pregnant women are encouraged to take prenatal vitamins, to eat healthful foods, and to avoid consuming products (such as alcohol and caffeine) that might harm their unborn child. Given the importance placed on food and nutrition, it is not surprising that the vast majority—73 percent—of moms of children of all ages believe they are changing the way their family eats to be more healthy versus the previous year.[1]

From a marketing perspective, food providers spend considerable effort to convince mom that she is making good nutritional choices for her child(ren), and they also offer mom convenient choices that her children will actually consume (i.e., child will not reject). We have found that while most moms are trying to provide a healthy diet for their child, the definition of "healthy diet" does vary considerably. While there is general agreement among many moms on important parts of nutrition, such as fruits, vegetables, and whole grains, there is often considerable variation in practice. This variation is driven by several factors, including whether the child is a picky eater or has a medical/health issue related to diet, the age of the child, factors such as access to fresh fruits and vegetables, cultural preferences, and importantly, mom's food preferences and dietary and nutrition concerns for herself (not just for her child).

As an example, the topic of getting their children to eat enough vegetables looms large in many conversations with moms. Many moms claim to have trouble getting their children to readily eat enough vegetables. The strategy of "hiding" vegetables in other products so that kids cannot taste them has moved well beyond homemade recipes to successful commercial products like YoBaby Meals (yogurt, fruit, and cereal combinations that are offered in flavors like pear and green beans, apple and sweet potato, or peach and squash) or Pirate's "Veggie Booty," which are snack puffs made from a mix of vegetables—including kale, spinach, and carrots—in addition to the primary ingredients of rice and corn. These products can be a "win-win" for mom if her child likes the taste and readily eats the product. While enjoying these foods, the child is also consuming the vegetables, which is mom's primary concern.

Fruits and vegetables are a key focus and an important part of many moms' definition of a healthy diet. In fact, almost half of moms (43 percent) reported that they are eating or serving more fruits and vegetables in their homes in 2010 when compared with the past, and the balance reported serving the same amount (49 percent). Only 8 percent of moms reported eating or serving less fruits and vegetables than in the past.[2] Additionally, as far as a fruit or a vegetable goes, every type counts for many moms. In fact, 53 percent find that "there is no difference to me—a vegetable is a vegetable; I just want my kids to eat it."[3]

It is also clear that some of the child's food preferences mirror those of mom, while others are distinct to the child's own taste preferences. For instance, if a mom is convinced that she does not like the taste of squash, it may be far easier to convince her to buy products for her children that contain squash disguised with other flavors than it will be to convince her to buy a product that is primarily squash or squash-flavored. Companies are well aware of this preference spillover from mom to child (sometimes called "habituation") and thus offer products that cater to mom's preferences.

In addition to fruits and vegetables, other important nutritional considerations that moms look to increase in their children's diets include (1) vitamin and mineral fortification and (2) natural, all-natural, or organic ingredients. In contrast, moms look to avoid or reduce high-fructose corn syrup, high sugar content, and artificial sweeteners.[4]

There are also several food areas that are equally important to moms for themselves and for their children. These include the highly popular area of whole grains, as well as the more specific concerns of gluten-free and lactose-free foods.[5]

When focused on their own diets, some moms' concerns shift more to keeping calories, fat, carbohydrate, and sodium content low.[6] Often, if mom finds a product that addresses her own special diet issues, she will use this for her family, as Mickey's comments illustrate:

> I have celiac [disease], so I have to be completely gluten-free in everything. I was diagnosed six years ago. Betty Crocker came out with a gluten-free cake mix—chocolate and yellow, cookie mix, and brownie mix. And on her Web site, she has different recipes. I used yellow cake mix and made carrot cake out of it for my family.
>
> ~ *Mickey, mom of a toddler*

Additionally, if mom approaches her own diet with weight management concerns, this can spill over to her child's diet, even with very young children. A recent example from qualitative interviews documented in February 2010 is that some moms were projecting their own weight concerns onto their infant and toddler daughters and were, therefore, restricting certain foods for these young girls, even if the pediatrician had found that the child's weight was appropriate.[7] We found moms are concerned with healthful food and weight-conscious diets for themselves across all age of child subgroups; however, moms of young adults and moms of teenagers were qualitatively even more concerned about their own weight management than other subgroups.

Several brands have capitalized on the insight that mom's focus on food and nutrition shifts as her child ages.

Infants/Toddlers

The infant/toddler years are a time of mom's intense focus on her child's diet, as well as a time of numerous physical and dietary transitions for her child, all condensed into a short period of time.

For a breast-feeding mom of a normal, healthy newborn, her own breast milk is generally recommended as the best diet, barring any complications or issues that prevent breast-feeding. However, by the time the child is three months old, many moms will select formula feeding either to supplement their breast-feeding or to replace it. As her child grows and mom introduces baby cereal and solid foods, she will often run into additional challenges that require compromises. For instance, she may find that the impact of her child's digestive system (e.g., gluten intolerance, lactose intolerance) and taste preferences may force trade-offs in the child's feeding regimen. In keeping with the constant balance that moms face between the ideal diet and the reality of what their child will eat, moms we interviewed also told us that they are more concerned with the "ideal" nutrition for a very young infant than for an older toddler or a preschooler.[8]

With the goal of a high-quality, healthful diet in mind, it is challenging for infant/toddler moms to consistently provide the desired nutrition in light of busy schedules, picky eaters, food allergies, budget challenges, and even mom's own food preferences and concerns that she projects onto her children. If mom is blessed with a child who is not a fussy eater, she may find that she can achieve the healthful diet goal fairly readily. However, if the child has medical conditions or is a picky eater, mom must decide how many battles to fight over food with her child. The choice to pick a battle goes against the emotional satisfaction that a mom receives when her child enjoys his or her food and readily eats.

As the child grows older, mom can obtain enhanced emotional satisfaction and bonding from other interactions with her child in addition to feeding her child. A sizable group of moms of older babies and toddlers that we spoke with recently said that they would rather spend time playing with or reading and singing to their child than fight a battle of perfect nutrition with the high-chair occupant. These moms still valued the soothing aspects of breast-feeding or bottle-feeding, but they also enjoyed the time to read to their children, play with them, and encourage their young child's gross motor skills development.[9] Mickey's comments illustrate how hard ensuring a nutritious diet can be for a toddler mom of a picky eater:

> My toddler is more picky about what he eats. He's weird about textures. He prefers purees. He was spitting out and refusing to eat. I will usually feed him the same thing as the older boys, and they basically all sit together. He'll eat a little on his own, then protest. . . . He wants pudding (smooth texture) or Gerber toddler foods.
>
> ~ *Mickey, mom of a toddler*

While infant/toddler moms are highly focused on their child's food intake, they also are facing intense parenting demands and limited time. We can see evidence of their struggles in several ways. For instance, moms of infants/toddlers are almost 50 percent more likely than moms on average to use quick-service/fast-food restaurants more often when compared with the prior year.[10] This may be because the demands of caring for an infant or a toddler create greater necessity for convenience.

Infant/toddler moms may also be managing their own weight, as Zola's comments illustrate:

> I am working on cutting out soda pop and creamer in my coffee. I am cutting that out for weight issues. I have not been able to lose my baby weight at all. I have put on five pounds in the past two years, and it's hard.

~ Zola, mom of an infant/toddler

There is an opportunity for brands that help infant/toddler moms during this busy, challenging life stage by providing convenient, nutritious food and beverage products that fit the families' lifestyles and also have tastes and forms that are appealing to the infant/toddler's palate. YoBaby Meals is a good example of a product line that offers nutrition, portion control, and convenience. Other good examples can be found in a range of toddler snack and meal products offered by Gerber Graduates and Beech-Nut's Let's Grow.

Preschoolers

In the preschool age range, the working situation of moms is highly polarized. Broadly speaking, there are two groups of moms of preschoolers: working and homemakers. This is not meant to suggest that homemakers are not working, rather that they are not being paid to perform tasks unrelated to caring for their home and family. According to the *State of the American Mom (SOAM)* estimates, 34 percent of moms of preschoolers work full time outside the home, and another 13 percent work part time outside the home or are self-employed. In addition, another 7 percent of moms are looking for work. This means approximately 50 percent of moms of preschoolers are employed outside the home, most of which is full time. In contrast, 38 percent of these moms are homemakers. The remaining balance of moms are students, retired, or not employed and not looking for work.[11]

While both working and homemaker moms of preschoolers have a shared value of the importance of healthful food and diet for their children (68 percent of working preschool moms rate healthy food and diet for their children as very important compared with 69 percent for homemaker preschool moms), their daily lives lead to different choices both at home and away from home.[12] A food or restaurant brand that offers mom an affordable, healthful option that her preschool child easily and readily consumes addresses a high priority for these moms.

When eating away from home, moms of preschoolers use more (13 percent of preschool moms versus 10 percent of total) or the same amount of quick-service/fast-food restaurants when compared with last year (54 percent of preschool moms versus 53 percent for total moms).[13] When looking at specific fast-food restaurant brands, moms of preschoolers are most likely to eat at McDonald's (76 percent of preschool moms versus 72 percent of total, and 68 percent of moms of infants/toddlers). Several other leading fast-food restaurants known for fries and hamburgers also do well with this segment, including Burger King, Wendy's, and Arby's. In addition, pizza chains overperform with moms of preschoolers, including Pizza Hut, Papa John's, and Domino's Pizza. Dunkin' Donuts also is visited on an above-average basis by moms of preschoolers. In contrast, two other leading quick-service restaurants, Subway and Taco Bell, both significantly underperform with these moms.[14] This is likely because preschool children do not as readily consume sub-style sandwiches and spicy food. These brand skews suggest that the food preferences of preschool children are influencing the mom's choice of restaurant. In addition, the ability of a preschool child to sit patiently in a restaurant setting is limited, as is his or her patience to stand in line at a restaurant while waiting to be seated. For these reasons, moms of preschoolers may further curtail the family's restaurant options to establishments that offer immediate seating, fast service, and distracting entertainment like coloring, puzzles, and video games at the table.

For approximately 50 percent of preschool children, some sort of day care arrangement (whether in a home or another setting) is part of their weekday life while mom works. In order to take a child to day care outside of the home and also to get the parent to work on time, the mom (or dad) must get the child up, dressed, and fed (more or less). This places clear time constraints on the breakfast occasion, and it also highlights the need for portable foods that mom can give to her preschool child to eat in transit. Alternatively, mom may rely on the day care or preschool provider to give

her child breakfast. Some day care centers and schools with preschool programs open their doors for drop-offs as early as 7 a.m., and with workdays
ending at 5 p.m., "after care" can extend as late as 7 p.m. in these settings.
In terms of food and nutrition, the mom may provide snacks, but often the
lunch menu is in the hands of the day care provider, not the parent. Din-
nertime at home also faces time constraints, given the early bedtimes of
most preschoolers and the fact that they (and their parents) are hungry after a long day. The challenges for moms in preparing a nutritious, healthy
family dinner after a full workday are significant. Similarly, there is a real
lack of time to prepare additional menu items if the child rejects the family
meal items. Often then, moms may opt for quick, family-pleasing favorites
with acceptable nutritional content, such as pasta with butter or marinara
sauce or breaded chicken pieces at home. Bonita's thoughts on dinner provide a good illustration of a working mom's approach in making sure her
son consumes enough fruits and vegetables in his diet.

> We eat dinner together as a family. I try to get him to eat. He gets dis-
> tracted at day care and doesn't necessarily eat as much as he should,
> and I want to make sure he gets enough to eat. We try to do lots of veg-
> etables. He likes cooked vegetables, and at day care there might only
> be raw [vegetables]. I try to get everything into him at night. Also, for
> fruit. I know they do some sort of fruit in the morning at day care, but
> I want to make sure he gets it. The individual cups of fruit or apple-
> sauce are perfect because he likes it that he gets his own cup, and we
> [adults] don't eat fruit at dinner.

~ Bonita, mom of a preschooler

We found a number of differences between working moms and homemaker
moms when it comes to their food choices for preschool children. For instance, when compared with homemaker moms with preschoolers, working
moms perceive that their preschool children are much more likely to specifically request the family choice of restaurant. When it comes to the restaurant
that is chosen, both working and homemaker moms of preschoolers agree
on McDonald's. Working moms of preschoolers are also twice as likely to
state that they eat out regularly as a way of managing their busy schedule.[15]

On the home front and in the grocery store, working moms of preschoolers differ from homemaker moms on a number of dimensions. The
working moms are less likely to perceive their children specifically asking
for "healthful" foods (11 percent versus 18 percent) and more likely to perceive requests for "treats" such as cookies, snacks, and cupcakes (32 percent

versus 22 percent), or ice cream and frozen novelties (31 percent versus 27 percent). Working moms of preschoolers are also more likely to perceive their child's request for juice/juice drinks (32 percent versus 21 percent) when compared with homemaker moms. Despite the hectic nature of their lives, in 2009, working moms of preschoolers reported that they were preparing more home-cooked meals (57 percent) when compared with the prior year. This is ahead of homemaker moms (52 percent), perhaps because they already prepared more home-cooked meals prior to the recession. Working moms of preschoolers also reported serving more fruits and vegetables in 2009 compared with 2008 (51 percent), ahead of homemaker moms (40 percent).[16]

While "pester power" is important to both segments, the working moms are more likely to notice their children's requests directly and to heed them when compared with the homemaker moms. While this might make it seem that working moms are more indulgent, it could also be the case that homemaker moms are automatically including their child's preferences in their decisions with less conscious recognition. We have seen this dynamic when moms buy particular brands of cookies, such as Oreos, knowing that their child likes the brand, without the child having to request the item directly.

Sara Lee Soft & Smooth is a case study that illustrates how a brand was built by successfully addressing the disconnect between the nutritional desire of moms to get more whole grains into their children's diets and the taste preferences of small children, including preschoolers and elementary school children who prefer a softer, smoother bread. More recently, in November 2010, Grupo Bimbo SAB bought Sara Lee's bakery business in North America.[17] The approach to meeting both mom and her child's needs continues for Soft & Smooth under the Grupo Bimbo ownership.

From a marketing perspective, given the high incidence of both homemaker and working moms, a brand can choose to develop messages and programs that appeal to both groups (as Soft & Smooth and McDonald's have both clearly done), or to select one of the two subgroups as its primary focus. A brand whose product is typically used by homemaker moms may elect to focus more on this segment. In contrast, working moms may be more open to direct messaging about how a restaurant makes the eating experience enjoyable and affordable for families.

Sara Lee Soft & Smooth

CASE STUDY

Sara Lee Soft & Smooth is a brand that has reached moms through its strategic partnerships and through its emphasis on providing nutritious products within the bread category. While traditionally associated with taste and indulgence instead of nutrition, the Sara Lee brand was able to tie its equity to nutrition through its innovations. Specifically, in 2005, Sara Lee launched Soft & Smooth Whole Grain White Bread to appeal to white bread lovers who were interested in getting the nutrition of whole grains while maintaining the texture of white bread. The white bread taste, appearance, and soft texture were particularly important to moms who faced resistance from their children when it came to eating coarser texture breads. These moms wanted the whole grains, but not the battle. To support this position, the introductory marketing campaign depicted children looking in the bread for the whole grains with a magnifying glass with no success. The product was the first broadscale offering that solved this problem, and Sara Lee was rewarded with strong results.

Starting with estimated sales of $56 million in 2006, the Sara Lee Soft & Smooth brand grew to $251 million in sales in 2008.[18] The company also invests efficiently in targeted marketing to promote the Soft & Smooth brand. [19] Sara Lee increased the impact of its marketing by using a partnership with Disney's *High School Musical 3: Senior Year* to appeal to moms. In this partnership, Sara Lee Soft & Smooth focused on Disney vehicles, including the Disney Channel, Disney.com, and a microsite. This strategy was effective for the brand because the Disney Channel was the most co-watched mom and kid network, while Disney.com was the most co-visited mom and kid Web site.[20] Hence, Sara Lee Soft & Smooth was able to engage with both moms and their children by appealing to children's desire for entertainment and mom's need for nutritious options.

The innovative product and the high-visibility marketing campaign helped propel the Sara Lee bread brand to the number one position in the U.S. with 8.8 percent market share, according to IRI data on September 21, 2008.[21] This tie-in was integral to some of the company's gains in the bread category, according to Sara Lee.[22] This is a

Sara Lee (continued)

good example of how a company can leverage the power of partner brands in order to reach a critical segment of moms by tying in with entertainment vehicles that can appeal to both moms and children. It is also a good example of how the product itself met the needs of both moms and their children, leading to success.

Elementary Schoolchildren

With the start of kindergarten and then elementary school, an overwhelming majority of children (96 percent or more) will spend many hours each day away from home in a school setting, regardless of the mom's working status. Despite home schooling's growth, only 2.9 percent of school-age children in the United States were homeschooled in 2007.[23]

For a mom who worked during her child's preschool years, elementary school is a continuation of the food preparation lifestyle that includes taking her child to a preschool setting or day care, where the child consumes at least one meal and often a snack away from home. In contrast, for a homemaker mom, the elementary school transition represents a new lifestyle where she is no longer able to monitor her child's lunch and snack intake as precisely as she could when the child was at home. In addition, the need to either carry a lunch to school or eat from the school's options sets constraints on the meal that did not exist when lunch was served at home.

Regardless of mom's working status, her elementary school-age child typically also exerts more control over his or her food choices than a pre-school-age child does. Thus, for the mom of an elementary schoolchild, there is less ability to control or influence the child's lunch food intake. In addition to child food and taste preferences, eating in the elementary school setting may require faster eating (to meet time constraints) or may result in distracted eating (as a school lunchroom is a busy place). Additionally, the practices of throwing food away or trading food can be common among elementary schoolchildren so that a mom cannot be certain that her child is eating the lunch or snack she provides. If the mom opts for the school-provided lunch for her child, the meal may represent a balanced nutritional perspective, but only if the child consumes the lunch as designed rather than just eating the portions that he or she prefers.

While some elementary schoolchildren bring a lunch made by their mom (or other caregiver) to school, there is another group of moms who rely on school lunches to feed their children. These school lunches are another source of concern for moms, according to a recent parent study by the W. K. Kellogg Foundation. This study found that more than half of parents perceive the nutritional quality of school lunches to be either "poor" or "only fair."[24]

While some moms may opt to become the lunchroom monitor in an attempt to stay on top of lunch at school, as a practical matter most moms will opt to focus more of their nutritional attention on dinner as the main meal of the day. The promise that dinner holds for moms is significant. Dinner is the chance for the child to eat their vegetables (sometimes the only chance), to receive a hot meal (since this may not be possible at school lunch), and to emotionally connect with mom and other family members. While family dinners are under siege due to after-school and evening activities, a majority of moms still place a high priority on eating dinner together as a family. In reality, given lunch away from home and the time pressure at breakfast as children are getting ready to go to school, dinner is the best weekday opportunity for the family to connect over a meal. The net result of these lifestyle demands are brands that recognize mom's efforts and success (even if idealized) of bringing the family together at dinner are delivering a message that will resonate with moms.

Quantitatively, dinner is identified as important to moms. In fact, a recent report from Babycenter.com reports that half of moms say dinner is the time they reconnect with the family, yet at the same time, two-thirds also find it to be the most challenging meal of the day.[25]

As a total segment, moms of elementary schoolchildren state that their children are important to the family's choice of restaurant (65 percent of moms of elementary schoolchildren state their child provides input), and this represents an increase of 16 points when compared with preschool moms (49 percent).[26]

The increased impact of elementary school children on family restaurant choice is driven by increases in child input for casual dining, whereas the rates of child influence in fast food are comparable between preschool and elementary school. This means that a casual dining or fine dining restaurant chain needs to obtain active elementary schoolchild endorsement to win more of the family's restaurant dollar.[27] Corkey's comments about the International House of Pancakes Restaurant (IHOP) illustrate this:

> Our family's favorite place is IHOP. We might go once a week, and Dakota [her eight-year-old son] likes to go. They have a coloring page with crayons or different promotions where the kids eat free. Dakota can choose the food he is in the mood for; it could be breakfast or cheeseburger and fries. We normally go there Friday night when I get off work. A couple times we haven't gone and Dakota has complained.

~ Corkey, mom of elementary schoolchild

When it comes to eating at home and grocery store food and beverage choices, moms of elementary schoolchildren perceive an increased influence of their children, with 52 percent saying their children request treats such as cookies, snacks, and cupcakes, up from 46 percent among moms of preschool children. The most striking increase is seen in the child's requests for soda, with 40 percent of moms of elementary schoolchildren recognizing that their child is providing input on this decision, nearly double the level of input of preschool-age children at 22 percent. As context, moms of elementary schoolchildren accept more input from their children on decisions across several categories and domains beyond food, including movies, clothing, extracurricular activities, and school supplies.[28] Elementary school moms expect more child input and involvement, and the food area is no exception.

Beyond input and influence on their moms' spending, elementary schoolchildren are significant consumers in their own right for specific categories of interest, including foods and beverages. Around 30 percent of moms of elementary schoolchildren report that their children spend their own money on ice cream/frozen novelties, juice/juice drinks, chips/crackers, treats such as cookies, snacks, and cupcakes, and candy/gum.[29]

In fact, James McNeal, Professor Emeritus of Marketing at Texas A&M University and author of more than eighty articles and five books focused on children's consumer behavior, estimated the spending power of children ages four to twelve at $7 billion of their own money in snacks in the year 2000.[30] This spending of the child's own money represents an important step toward independence, but it also illustrates the fact that mom is controlling and influencing a smaller portion of her child's diet. Given the purchasing power of elementary schoolchildren, as well as their "pester power," we observe a mix of marketing strategies by food and restaurant companies in choosing to target either mom, the child, or both. There are many considerations, including regulations, that go into this decision, and this requires considerable examination on the part of the organization.

A final major area of elementary schoolchildren's diet is after-school snacks. It is common for an elementary schoolchild to have a snack after school, either at home or in transit, if they have a sports practice or other extracurricular activity. Typically the mom purchases these snacks at a grocery store. From the mom's standpoint, the ideal after-school snack will fill her child up enough to last until dinner, but not fill her child so much that he or she is no longer hungry enough to eat a full dinner. As we have discussed, dinner perhaps is the most important meal of the day emotionally and nutritionally to mom, and so the snack plays a complementary role. While breakfast is also considered very important nutritionally, it does not have the shared family experience in many households and is thus slightly less important emotionally than dinner. As a result, we have found that many moms are less demanding on the nutritional or health qualities of the snack, since they view it as a small, ancillary player in the diet. There is a demand for healthy snacks among moms, but less nutritious alternatives like cookies and crackers are considered acceptable by many moms given the limited role the snack is perceived to play (though many may draw the line at a candy bar). Yolanda's focus on getting her son to consume fruits and vegetables illustrates this point.

> It's the fruits and vegetables; I am always trying to push them. He loves the V8 V-Fusion, and they come in a carryable size.... Fruitables [made by Apple & Eve] are also good. My mother-in-law reinforces the fruit as a snack also.
>
> ~ *Yolanda, mom of elementary schoolchild*

In summary, the elementary school years encompass a massive change on the mom's part when it comes to control over her child's food and nutrition choices. While the focus is generally on marketing to moms at this age range, brands also need to consider the child's input in the decisions. For instance, casual dining restaurants must get the child's vote to win with this age range and need to offer choices that appeal to and entertain elementary schoolchildren. IHOP provides an example of a casual dining restaurant that appeals to this age group.

Middle Schoolers

In the middle school years, mom continues to maintain a strong focus on healthy diet for her child. One of mom's main approaches is to provide healthy food options for the meals eaten at home. As with the other age groups, moms often will use quick meals at home as a way to juggle the family's busy lifestyle. In addition, moms increasingly ask their teenagers and middle schoolers to help share in the household chores (64 percent of moms of teens ask children to help with household chores, up from 49 percent of moms with children ages seven to twelve).[31] One of the household chores that these middle schoolers are asked to help with is cooking and food preparation.

In addition to meal preparation, in some households that we have visited, specifically Hispanic households where the parents both work, teenagers and middle schoolers may also help by doing some of the grocery shopping. This goes beyond the child providing mom with input, to the child being the person who actually takes on responsibility for part of the food shopping. As a result, when it comes to food decisions for middle school children at home, these Hispanic middle schoolers and teenagers can have an even more influential role on household spending.

An example of a food product that has been specifically designed to meet the nutritional needs of elementary and middle schoolchildren is Barilla PLUS pasta. The product is designed to have a taste profile similar to regular pasta, so it is appealing to the family's taste preferences. In addition to taste, Barilla PLUS also delivers more protein than many multigrain pastas (10 grams of protein for a 210 calorie serving, compared to 5 grams of protein for Trader Joe's or Whole Foods multigrain offerings).[32] Using Barilla PLUS pasta, a mom or her middle schoolchild can easily make a quick family pasta dinner for a school night that the entire household will enjoy. In this way, moms can give their children more nutrition in a food they typically love. The Barilla PLUS case study is a good example of a product that succeeds by meeting adults' nutritional needs and children's taste preferences.

In addition to the household spending that they influence, middle schoolers also have their own discretionary funds to spend. While these children continue to use their own funds for treats and snacks, we also see a huge increase in the use of their own money to buy soda. The number increases from 4 percent among moms of children ages seven to twelve who report their child buys soda with their own money to 16 percent of moms of

Barilla PLUS

Food brands can leverage the importance moms place on healthy food/diet for their children to create brand loyalty among this integral segment. Companies can drive sales by introducing innovative products that address moms' unmet needs in feeding their children.

In 2005, Barilla America introduced a line of healthy multigrain pasta called Barilla PLUS in order to reach these nutritionally minded moms. Barilla provided these moms with an innovative, tasty food product and positioned it as a way moms could incorporate fiber and other nutrients into their family's daily meals. Kamal Dagher, vice president of product development at Barilla, said, "We wanted to deliver balanced nutrition that would satisfy the most demanding dieticians and nutritionists, and with taste, texture and color that would satisfy the most finicky kids. We knew that the combination of these two benefits is what made the project very difficult to achieve. At the same time, we also knew that achieving both benefits is what makes the project worthwhile."[33] PLUS was designed to be rich in important nutrients like protein, fiber, and Omega-3's.[34] This strategy of offering moms convenient solutions to feed their children helped Barilla succeed in its introduction of Barilla PLUS. As of 2008, PLUS was a $50 million business in the United States.[35] PLUS is also successful in that it commands a substantial price premium over ordinary pasta—almost $1 per box. For example, as of May 11, 2011, the Peapod Web site offered Barilla PLUS Angel Hair Multigrain on sale at $2.59 for a 14.5-ounce box as compared to the regular Barilla Angel Hair pricing of $1.79 for a 16-ounce box.[36]

As a further convenience, the PLUS product offers mom the added simplicity of not having to include any extra ingredients to make a wholesome meal. For instance, if the product is served just with butter or olive oil, it still delivers protein, and the mom does not have to add a meat dish such as chicken to the meal. This approach of positioning Barilla PLUS as an innovative way to provide children a meal in and of itself helped make the product launch successful for Barilla's U.S. business.

CASE
STUDY

Barilla PLUS (continued)

Barilla was able to create a product and tailor it directly to its target consumers. As a result, the company gave moms the choice of a convenient, nutritious solution for their children's meals. Barilla PLUS is a good example of a successful innovation that met the needs of moms.

children ages thirteen to seventeen. In the candy and gum category, there is also a large increase, up from 15 percent of moms of children ages seven to twelve to double that level at 31 percent of moms of children ages thirteen to seventeen.[37] Eleanor's story of her son's candy binge illustrates this point:

> My two top concerns for him are nutrition and academics. He doesn't like a lot of foods; he is a picky eater and won't take any initiative to get food for himself. He won't even heat up a frozen pizza or a frozen dinner. A good example is that he wasn't hungry for dinner the other night. I asked if he had a snack. It turned out that he bought a giant bag of gummy Life Savers on his way home and ate the entire bag, which was seven hundred fifty calories.

> *~ Eleanor, mom of a middle schooler and a young adult*

A challenge for moms of middle schoolers is to continue to reinforce healthy eating habits and better choices for their children, in light of the less than healthy choices that moms recognize their children make when the children spend their own money. Moms will welcome brands and other organizations (e.g., schools, community groups) that help reinforce the healthy eating message. There is an opportunity to communicate this message in a way that will capture the interest and attention of middle schoolers as well, such as through videos, games, or songs.

Teenagers

By the time their oldest child hits the teenage years, many moms have returned to work full time (an estimated 40 percent of moms of teens are employed full time). In addition, 22 percent of moms of teens work part time or are self-employed, bringing the estimated percent of moms of teens who work to almost two-thirds (62 percent). The family lifestyle then includes a working mom, and a teen child who spends the vast majority of the weekday hours at school and/or in extracurricular activities outside of the home.[38] Busy teen lifestyles with late afternoon extracurriculars also place further limits on mom's impact on food choices for her teen. Despite her diminished influence on her teen's diet, mom still attempts to provide her teen with good choices and also to support the child with healthful options. At times, teen weight concerns are also addressed by the mom. Marly's story about her teen son illustrates this involvement:

> He's six-foot-four-inches tall, and he weighed two hundred twenty-five pounds. He was playing both junior varsity and varsity football with two games a week. There were issues, and one of the seniors said to him, "If you weren't so slow and fat we would have won." So he went on a starvation diet and got down to one hundred ninety pounds. Since then, he has stabilized and wants to gain weight for football in a healthy way. He reads labels, and if it's more than one hundred calories from fat he won't touch it. So I have to be more creative with my cooking because healthy food is more expensive. He won't even eat baked fries now. He loves paninis. Target had a panini maker on sale, and I bought it for him. I bake the chicken, and he makes his own sandwiches with the panini maker using the chicken. During the summer when I'm at work during the day, he uses his panini maker each day.
>
> *~ Marly, mom of a teenager*

From a marketing perspective, the traditional wisdom in these age ranges is to focus on the teen directly, and marketing to the mom is often avoided for fear of alienating the teen. This traditional approach remains popular despite considerable evidence that the current teens (the Millennials) are a group that is highly engaged with their parents.

As an example of this closeness and mutual influence, we have heard anecdotal accounts of Millennial teenagers' eating practices influencing their parents. For instance, one teenage daughter became a pescetarian, and ultimately her mom followed suit. An example of a mom influencing teen choices is found in an Asian American family with two teenage children that makes a point of having at least one dinner each week with Asian food to reinforce their cultural heritage with their children.

For restaurants, I find a lot of value in Asian foods. There has to be two to three meals a week that are Japanese, in a restaurant or at home, or any kind of noodle dish.

~ Karly, Asian mom of two teenagers

From a promotional standpoint, there is an opportunity for an organization to sponsor a mom and teen cooking contest. The contest could encourage family ties by showcasing traditional family favorites along with new traditions that the family has just discovered, or it could turn the tables by having the teen introduce mom to a new dish. This would build on the practice of many local organizations and youth groups that encourage teens to bring a family favorite dish to a "potluck" night to encourage trying new foods and to celebrate family diversity.

We recognize that some organizations will decide that the most effective approach for their product or service in the food area will be to focus solely on the teen. We believe, however, that for other organizations there is an opportunity to leverage food to celebrate the parent/teen relationship or to celebrate cultural and family traditions. This opportunity can go beyond food and restaurant brands to other organizations given food's saliency and wide appeal.

Young Adults

When young adults leave the family home, mom's direct influence on food choices is further curtailed. For young adults who leave the home to go to college, freshmen weight gain of several pounds is considered typical given the lack of parental control and a multitude of food options available in college dining plans. In contrast, for mom there may be more time available to focus on her own diet to make both healthful and weight-conscious choices when her child is a young adult.

Even though young adults who continue to live at home experience more direct mom impact on their food choices, these young adults still bring personal groceries and food selections into the family refrigerator or pantry. In addition, young adult schedules and lifestyles may not sync up with mom or the rest of the family, so they may not consistently participate in family meals.

Basic cooking skills, information on preparing nutritious meals, and knowledge of appropriate portion control guidelines are frequently lacking among young adults. As a result, young adults will often look to mom as a trusted resource on how to prepare a dish, select ingredients, or follow a recipe. For instance, one mom we know e-mailed her daughter, who was living abroad, highly detailed recipes and instructions to help her to prepare family favorite dishes. As a young adult in college, Nicole provides an example of frequently seeking her mom's input on food choices:

> My mom and I are really, really close. When it comes to food, she knows about this stuff. I definitely call her and ask her about getting the right nutrients and vitamins. And also about calories and cholesterol. It was hard eating at the college cafeteria, no way to tell about calories. Also, I have food allergies, and I will call her to see if I can eat it [some specific food]. My mom researched my soy and olive oil food allergy more than me. Now I'm home on break from college, we cook together all the time.

> *~ Nicole, nineteen-year-old college student*

As with teens, there continues to be an opportunity to recognize the importance of mom's influence with her young adult children in the area of food and nutrition. Alicia's story about modeling healthful eating for her young adult daughter is a good example:

> When Ashlee first came home from college, she wanted to have all of her favorites like egg rolls and chicken fried rice. We did that at first, and then I let her know I'm going back to eating healthy. A goal is the healthy eating for my daughters. If they see me doing it, they see the effects on me overall. I can see the difference in myself, and I definitely tell my daughters. For instance, my skin was getting breakouts from the fried foods, and my feet couldn't fit into my shoes from swelling from all the salt I was eating.

> *~ Alicia, mom of young adults*

Alicia also mentioned that a local youth group helped educate her college-age daughter on healthful eating by teaching her daughter to read ingredient labels. In Alicia's words, "It took someone else to tell her [to get the point across]." This suggests a major opportunity for organizations that work with young adults to support mom by providing their children with healthful eating tips served up in an age-relevant manner.

Conclusion

In summary, the topic of food and mom's influence is a rich area for brand leaders. Food as a theme commands high interest that can be used by a wide

Food

THEME RESOURCE GUIDE

	Mom's Concern For Her Child	Mom's Concern For Herself
Infant/Toddler Moms	• Good overall nutrition and developing broad taste palate	• Weight management or loss
Preschool Moms	• "Healthy," fruits and vegetables, avoid excess sugar	• Weight management or loss
Elementary School Moms	• "Healthy," fruits and vegetables • Fuel for the day	• Weight management
Middle School Moms	• Dinner focus • Encourage healthy choices	• Weight management
Moms of Teens	• Encourage healthy on-the-go choices	• Weight management
Moms of Young Adults	• Recipe and cooking advice • Guidance on better choices	• Weight management

▓ = Higher Mom's priority
▓ = Moderate Mom's priority
▓ = Lower Mom's priority

variety of organizations. Several brands have enjoyed considerable success by offering food products to meet mom's and her child's needs and preferences. These include Sara Lee Soft & Smooth bread and Barilla PLUS pasta. Additionally, other brands, like McDonald's and IHOP, do a great job of appealing to both mom and her child for the family's restaurant dollars. While food and beverage manufacturers and restaurants focus a great deal of attention on mom's influence, nonfood organizations can also tap into this high involvement, emotional area. In particular, the area of supporting mom's goals of encouraging healthful food choices for older children (middle school and beyond) is a less explored opportunity area open to creative approaches. Moms will likely appreciate brands that support the message of the importance of healthful eating to their young adult child. An example of a practical message that a brand could deliver would be the findings from a 2000 study by Mickey T. Trockel, Michael D. Barnes, and Dennis L. Egget, who discovered that college students who ate breakfast had a higher first-year college grade point average.[39]

The Theme Resource Guide: Food is a tool that we have developed to enable a brand to quickly examine mom's priorities on the theme by age of child. It offers two perspectives: (1) Mom's Concerns for Her Child, and (2) Mom's Concern for Herself. For example, food is a higher priority during the child's infant/toddler years than it is for the child's young adult years. When mom does focus on food for her young adult child, it is with recipes and advice as well as guidance or better choice suggestions.

There is also an opportunity for brands to support mom's own diet, nutrition, and weight management goals. One brand that did a good job of this is Betty Crocker, which offers several gluten-free baking mixes as well as recipe ideas on their Web site that enable mom to deliver gluten-free treats that her whole family can enjoy.[40]

Notes

1. Marketing to Moms Coalition, *State of the American Mom* 2010.
2. Ibid.
3. Ibid.
4. Ibid.
5. Ibid.
6. Ibid.
7. Qualitative Interviews, Insight to Action, February 2010.

8. Ibid.

9. Ibid.

10. Marketing to Moms Coalition, *State of the American Mom* 2010.

11. Ibid., 2009.

12. Ibid.

13. Ibid., 2010.

14. Ibid., 2009.

15. Ibid.

16. Ibid.

17. Carlos Manuel Rodriguez and Matthew Boyle, "Grupo Bimbo to Buy Sara Lee Unit for $959 Million," Bloomberg, November 9, 2010, accessed May 14, 2011, http://www.bloomberg.com/news/2010-11-09/sara-lee-sells-north-american-fresh-bakery-to-grupo-bimbo-for-959-million.html.

18. Personal interview with Heather Collins, December 17, 2008.

19. Ibid.

20. Ibid.

21. Karlene Lukovitz, "Strong Q1 for Sara Lee, Including Bakery," November 5, 2008, accessed March 9, 2010, http://www.mediapost.com/publications/?fa=Articles.showArticle&art_aid=94179.

22. Ibid.

23. *USA Today*, "Home Schooling Grows," updated January 5, 2009, accessed May 14, 2011, http://www.usatoday.com/news/education/2009-01-04-homeschooling_N.htm.

24. W. K. Kellogg Foundation, "Americans want pizza, burgers and nuggets pulled from school menus, poll finds," April 28, 2010, accessed June 29, 2010, http://www.wkkf.org/news/Articles/2010/04/Americans-want-pizza-burgers-and-nuggets-pulled-from-school-menus-poll-finds.aspx.

25. Babycenter.com, "21st Century Mom," 2009, accessed May 14, 2011, http://www.babycentersolutions.com/downloads/Mom_Insights_Mealtime_Mom.pdf.

26. Marketing to Moms Coalition, *State of the American Mom* 2009.

27. Ibid.

28. Ibid.

29. Ibid.

30. James U. McNeal, *The Kids Market: Myths and Realities,* Ithaca: Paramount Market Publishing, Inc., 1999, 29.

31. Marketing to Moms Coalition, *State of the American Mom* 2009.

32. Elaine Magee, "A Healthier Bowl of Pasta: Whole-grain and higher-fiber pastas are healthier. But how do they taste?" accessed May 14, 2011, http://www.webmd.com/food-recipes/features/healthier-bowl-pasta.

33. Joan Holleran, "Formula 417: with Barilla Plus, Barilla reinvents pasta for the American consumer," February 1, 2006, accessed May 14, 2011, http://www.allbusiness.com/manufacturing/food-manufacturing/878669-1.html.

34. Barilla Plus Pasta, accessed May 14, 2011, http://www.barillaus.com/Pages/Product-Landing.aspx?brandID=5 accessed.

35. Personal Interview with Angela Goldberg, December 15, 2008.

36. Angel Hair Pasta (search results on Peapod Web site), accessed May 14, 2011, www. peapod.com.

37. Marketing to Moms Coalition, *State of the American Mom* 2009.

38. Ibid., 2010.

39. Mickey T. Trockel, Michael D. Barnes, and Dennis L. Egget, "Health-Related Variables and Academic Performance Among First-Year College Students: Implications for Sleep and Other Behaviors," *Journal of American College Health* 49(3): 125-31.

40. Betty Crocker Gluten Free, accessed May 14, 2011, http://www.betty-crocker.com/recipes/health-and-diet/gluten%20free.

CHAPTER 3

Exercise and Sports: Moving Together

Traditionally, mom's focus has included her child's physical safety, proper nutrition, character development, interpersonal skills, education, and other areas. In addition, sports, physical exercise, and fitness are receiving more focus from today's moms. In fact, many moms are highly involved in their children's sports programs. The evidence for this can be found on any Saturday or Sunday morning by observing local sports fields, which are full of moms watching their children compete. *State of the American Mom* (*SOAM*) research finds that physical exercise and fitness are a high priority for moms of children of all ages, ranking ninth out of the top ten priorities. In addition to physical exercise and fitness, sports programs for their children are also important to moms, especially for moms of children ages seven to seventeen.[1] Moms often are invested in their children's extracurricular activities, and sports are the leading pastime. Forty-nine percent of moms report that their children participate in sports as an extracurricular, well ahead of other areas like music (21 percent), art (15 percent), dance (15 percent), or theater (7 percent).[2]

Many moms are personally involved in their child's extracurricular activities, including sports and other forms of physical exercise such as dance. We often hear moms of elementary schoolchildren joking about how their lives are governed by their child's sports, and that they spend hours transporting their children to the programs. Beyond chauffeuring, many moms stay to watch the game (often) or practice (depending on schedule). Today, 40 percent of moms spend more than three hours a week attending their child's extracurricular activities, while another 38 percent spend up to three hours a week.[3] In the Evanston, Illinois, American Youth Soccer Organization (AYSO), it is not uncommon for at least one or both parents to attend every soccer game in their elementary schoolchild's schedule. Evanston AYSO games are typically held on the weekends. Attending weekend games becomes part of the family lifestyle, and mom begins to think of herself as the parent of an athletic child. Karly's observations are a good illustration of this dynamic:

> Sports are a physical necessity for him. It's also important for leadership and emotional stability. There is the physical chemistry of what happens when you are competing. He has to stay focused for teammates and himself and support the goals. There is a discipline transfer. My role is to "support his passion." I see myself as "football mom" because I feel his desires and support them. I am not a mom who is really afraid of injury—if this is his passion, part of it is that he will get an injury. There are many arenas to be involved in the sports world with your child. The child feels your total focus; you want the parent involved.

> ~ *Karly, mom of two teenagers*

Mom's involvement in her child's sports is common, particularly at the elementary school level. Our research finds that 60 percent of moms of children ages seven to twelve report their child participates in sports, well ahead of total moms at 49 percent, high school moms at 53 percent, or moms of children under six at 46 percent.[4] Sports are increasingly available for players of all talent levels, and parent and mom involvement is emphasized by leagues, and it is sometimes necessary in order for the children to participate. Mom can directly act as a coach or an assistant coach of the team, or she can contribute as the "team mom," who is responsible for coordinating snacks, the coach appreciation gift, and other duties. On Saturdays and Sundays, moms can spend a significant portion of the day driving to and attending games for their children. It is less common for many moms of elementary schoolchildren to drop their child off at a weekend game and leave the child alone at the sports activity. Instead, many moms attend the game and actively cheer on the sidelines or chat with other parents.

This combination of prioritizing sports as an extracurricular activity and the mom's acceptance of sports as an important part of the family lifestyle is a major trend in modern families. Often, sports provide more direct opportunities for mom involvement than the classroom, even though moms can certainly volunteer in the school.

From a marketing standpoint, this family lifestyle trend—with a strong focus on sports during the elementary school years—presents the opportunity to speak with mom and help support her with her child's extracurricular activities. Brands that focus on sports have long made sponsoring youth teams a priority, often to build a relationship with the child. For example, Nike supports both moms and their child athletes by offering customized equipment to both enhance performance (for the child) and promote safety (for the mom). Another marketing opportunity is for brands to connect with the team parent (often the mom) who plans the snacks, equipment pickup, coach appreciation gift, and end-of-season gathering.

For the youngest age ranges, such as infant/toddler and preschool, mom's focus is often more on her child being physically active and building gross motor skills. For the older children, specifically young adults and some teenagers, mom's primary focus will then shift back from sports to physical fitness and exercise. In addition, mom often has fitness and exercise goals for herself that brands and organizations can support.

Infants/Toddlers

The infant/toddler years are generally not associated with formal sports programs or "extracurriculars." In fact, 38 percent of moms of children under the age of six report no extracurriculars for their child, well ahead of other age groups. Still, 62 percent report at least one extracurricular.[5] There are a number of organized programs that encourage activity and physical fitness available to moms of infants and toddlers, including "Mommy and Me" classes, infant swim classes, gymnastics, dance, and others. Mom is often interested in these activities because of the expectation that child development broadly, and gross motor skills in particular (not just physical fitness), are enhanced through these types of experiences. For mom, these programs afford an opportunity for a child-friendly excursion outside of the home and even a potential opportunity to exchange tips or socialize with other moms of infants/toddlers. These additional benefits for mom combine with the child development and physical fitness benefits for her child.

In fact, *SOAM* research shows that moms of infants/toddlers view physical exercise and fitness as a high priority, ranking sixth in importance for these moms, as compared with ranking ninth for total moms. By comparison with total moms, moms of infants/toddlers correspondingly rank sports programs lower—as may be expected.[6] Thus, the focus for brands and marketers who are targeting infant and toddler moms is often more on encouraging physical activity than sports skills. Sports themes at these ages are probably more for the parent's benefit, as well as the parent's projection of his or her own sports interest on the child. In our experience, infant/toddler programs commonly use music to encourage movement rather than focusing on sports.

In addition to classes, there are many developmental "toys" marketed to moms who are hoping to encourage infant and toddler development. For example, there are several infant gyms actively on the market in 2011, including models from the Fisher-Price Rainforest brand that emphasizes music and lights along with toys. These toys are designed to encourage physical movement of infants who are not yet sitting or crawling. There are also several "gyms" that adapt to allow a child to be able to use it, initially on their back, and later while sitting. An example of this is the MGA 5-in-1 Adjustable Gym, about which some moms wrote favorable reviews on Amazon for the product's relevance to both infants and their older toddler siblings.[7]

Beyond gyms and toys, there is also a wide range of infant and toddler exercise DVDs, some intended for the moms as the primary viewer (e.g., *Yoga with Your Baby, Baby Builders*), and some intended for the toddler or preschooler as the ultimate audience (e.g., from *Sesame Street, Elmo's World— Food, Water & Exercise!*). The DVDs that enable mom to work out while "exercising" her infant/toddler child present a highly aspirational scenario for mom (although perhaps one that is unrealistic on a sustained basis).

Marissa's interest in setting a good role model for her two-year-old by exercising with videos is a good example of many moms' thoughts on this topic:

> I do think it's important to do exercise. . . . We want him to think it's a normal part of life, so when he's grown up he will work out. I'll do workout videos in front of my son and he'll try to do it with me—he'll try to do it and jump up and down. We're not the skinniest; we're not overweight. It will be helpful for him because being heavy runs in our family. My husband and me were both fat kids. Hopefully, we are giving him a better example.

> ~ *Marissa, mom of an infant/toddler*

For mom, her own physical fitness is often another important goal. This can be especially true for a mom of an infant/toddler who had a baby within the past two years. In fact, moms of infants/toddlers had higher rates of weekly participation in several exercise activities, including fitness walking (50 percent), cardiovascular exercise (34 percent), dance (23 percent), and fitness classes (16 percent), when compared with other mom age groups.[8]

Mom may need to get back in shape and want to lose weight and re-store her pre-baby figure. A wide variety of equipment such as baby joggers, strollers, bike trailers, and infant carriers can help mom with this goal while allowing her to spend time with the child. In addition to efforts on her own or at a gym, there are organized exercise groups for moms with strollers to do fitness walking together. Stroller Strides is an example of an organization that promotes working out together for moms of infants/toddlers.[9] Mar-keters can support moms through tie-ins with such organizations, and the LUNA brand is a good example of this with the LUNA Moms Club, pow-ered by Stroller Strides.[10]

Moms of infants/toddlers often are very open to brands, products, and services that help them support their goal of physical fitness and exercise for their child and for themselves. Mom's goal for her child at this age range cen-ters around gross motor skill development, in a focus we call "gross motor basics." Products and services that support mom in encouraging her child's gross motor basics development are attractive. In other cases, the product will directly support mom's own exercise interest. In addition, a brand can also form a creative partnership, such as the LUNA Moms Club, to achieve this goal and link to this high-priority area.

Preschoolers

During the preschool years, mom's child is able to perform somewhat more skilled physical activities. These physical activities can include a wide variety of exercise and sports-related areas ranging from dance, gymnastics, begin-ning sports such as T-ball, swimming, or skiing. Mom's choices are expanded in terms of the activities and "sports" programs that her child can try out and perhaps enjoy.

Playing outside with her child is the number one physical activity that moms of preschoolers most favor, with 77 percent of moms encouraging this approach. While casual outdoor play is popular, almost half of preschool moms also take the time to plan active family activities and trips.[11]

As an example of this, Park City Mountain Resort offers ski instruction for children ages three and a half to five, under its Signature 3 program. This program includes approximately two and a half hours of daily outdoors practice. For children that are able to demonstrate the necessary skills in the fenced-in training area, there is also a separate beginner area complete with ski lift where they will ski under closely supervised conditions.[12]

Luna

The LUNA brand was started in 1999 as a line of nutrition bars specifically designed for the needs of women, from the makers of Clif Bars.[13] The LUNA brand is promoted through a range of cause-related marketing tailored to particular hot-button areas for women. Some major areas that the brand has supported are women's filmmaking (LUNAFEST), the Breast Cancer Fund, and the LUNA Moms Club. The LUNA Moms Club is focused on helping moms of young children to be fit and active in a social way through a partnership with Stroller Strides. Alexa, a mom of an infant/toddler that we spoke with, raved about how beneficial she finds Stroller Strides, both physically and emotionally. In addition to supporting mom in being active, the LUNA Moms Club also has a charitable component with "Moms with a Mission" activities.[14]

A second way that LUNA supports moms (in addition to women in general) can be found in the "Who Inspires You?" section of the brand's Web site, which offers women a chance to share the story of an inspirational woman. Many of the postings are for moms from their adult female children. A typical posting follows:

> To My Mama Flora,
>
> Mom, you came to America 30+ years ago to start a new life. Now, twenty-seven years later, I am grown up and well educated. You are an inspiration to me and all the women who had the courage to fly to a foreign country and call it their home. You, as a single mom, also raised both my brother and I while working full time. I hope someday I will be just as courageous and strong just like you. I love you mom!!
>
> *~ Mae, May 11, 2011*[15]

With its focus on women, LUNA is an excellent example of a brand that has developed programs that connect specifically with moms and use this connection to drive its relevance, along with supporting women broadly.

During the preschool years, there are several factors that contribute to the choice of sports or fitness activity chosen for the child. These include local availability and convenience, mom and dad's own preferences, and fit with the family lifestyle. For instance, if the family spends its free time near oceans, rivers, pools, or lakes, mom will often place a higher priority on her child learning swimming for safety reasons. One mom we spoke to in Florida, for example, remarked that pediatricians in Florida emphasize swimming at a young age due to the proximity of pools and beaches. Additionally, if an older sibling participates in a particular sport, mom may elect to have her younger child participate in the same sport for practical reasons. Additionally, if the parents enjoy a particular activity like skiing, they will tend to select a family ski vacation that allows the group to participate in this pastime. Some families also focus on participating as fans of a particular sport that the parents are fond of, such as baseball. One family we know takes their sons to Yankees baseball games on a regular basis and also encourages them to play baseball. Thus, they are a "baseball family."

Bonita provides an example of the activity choice being driven by local access and convenience along with parental preference. Her three-year-old daughter participates in a "creative movement class."

> I try to keep her active all the time. My idea right now is putting her in ballet, creative movement, because she said she wants to do ballet. I picked this because I knew the park, since my sisters had done dance classes there, and it's close to our home. . . . Eventually I would like her to join T-ball or some soccer. . . . Personally, I like to dance, and my husband knows soccer.

> *~ Bonita, mom of preschooler*

Bonita's choice is shared by many other moms. In fact, we find that child dance participation is at its highest level in the preschool years, with 38 percent of moms reporting their child participates in a dance activity weekly.[16]

Beyond sports programs, dance, and outdoor play, there are also specific products and programs designed to encourage preschool fitness and exercise. One very interesting example of a product line that focuses on promoting exercise, which also allows mom and her child to mimic one another, comes from a brand called Redmon. Redmon USA offers a treadmill, exercise bike, and weight bench, among other "fun and fitness products for kids." While these items are listed as designed primarily for preschoolers age three to seven, online customer reviews for the mini-treadmill suggest that this product is being being used by both younger and older children as well, from toddlers to elementary schoolchildren.[17] Many preschool moms are focused on working out and exercising to stay healthy and avoid weight gain. These moms use treadmills and exercise bikes, both at home and at the gym. It may seem natural, then, for mom's preschool child to have similar equipment. In addition to the mini-treadmills, Redmon USA also recognizes the family sports weekend lifestyle by offering kid's camp chairs and a "Baby Beach Chair" with umbrella, perfect for children to sit in on the sidelines at their sibling's soccer game.[18]

As with moms of infants/toddlers, many moms of preschoolers also want to exercise and keep fit. Access to flexible child care that allows mom to work out is helpful as preschool children need supervision. Some gyms offer "family" memberships with babysitting services on-site. For example, the Lifetime Fitness chain delivers a family-friendly environment by offering two hours per day of infant care for children ages three to eleven months, and also two hours per day for children ages eleven months to eleven years.[19] Since Lifetime Fitness requires that mom remain on-site, she can exercise in the rest of the club, secure in the knowledge that her child is well cared for and that she will be paged if she is needed. Lifetime Fitness child care centers offer entertainment options such as climbing equipment, a basketball court, arts and crafts, and computer play.

During the preschool years, many of the fitness and exercise options that are selected are driven by family lifestyle factors and the mom's interests. Brands and marketers that recognize this dynamic and encourage mom in her goal of keeping her children active and supporting their skill development will be rewarded. Products and services that allow a child to imitate mom or dad's exercise and sports activities are popular. We call this focus "imitation." There is also the opportunity for brands to support mom in her own desire to remain active and fit.

Elementary Schoolchildren

Mom involvement is increasingly common in supporting child participation in sports during the elementary school years. Within this context of involvement, the elementary school years are the most active and the highest point for mom's direct participation. In fact, 48 percent of moms of elementary schoolchildren report spending more than three hours a week personally attending their child's extracurriculars, well ahead of total moms at 40 percent.[20] Additionally, as mentioned previously, 60 percent of moms of children ages seven to twelve report that their child participates in sports.[21] This high level of elementary child sports participation is found among both moms of girls (57 percent) and moms of boys (64 percent). There are a number of reasons behind this high level of mom participation, including the elementary child's more advanced physical skills, the natural stage of child development (versus greater separation of middle school and teen years), and the need of many elementary school sports leagues for parent volunteers in order to function. The need for parental help in the elementary school years, and to some extent during middle school, contrasts with many high school leagues that have paid coaching or coaching from a schoolteacher.

Today, in the elementary school years from a cultural standpoint, it seems almost that a mom who does not stay and attend her child's game makes a bigger statement than a mom who does attend. While on the sidelines watching her child's game, mom can also exchange tips about the best training, summer camps, sports equipment, snacks, and other factors related to sports. Gillian's spring family weekend schedule is an example of the demands of a sport's lifestyle on her family:

> With four boys, our family life on weekends revolves around the boys' sports schedule. This is particularly so during the spring season when they are playing both baseball and soccer. Every Friday evening, our one son has back-to-back soccer and baseball practices. On Saturday, we have two more soccer practices and two baseball games. On Sunday, we rush back from church so that all the boys can attend their afternoon soccer games. The logistics of getting all the boys where they need to be at the right time is staggering. We are glad the boys are involved in these team sports but sometimes it seems all-consuming.

~ *Gillian, mom of elementary schoolchildren and a middle schoolchild*

As further evidence of this involvement, sport leagues often now ask moms to monitor their sideline comportment and to sign a code of conduct to prevent unsportsmanlike behavior. Moms are educated on the importance of positive coaching. These actions by the leagues are in direct response to the high degree of parental involvement in their child's sports and to the negative behaviors that can arise when the parents become overly emotional on the sidelines. The Positive Coaching Alliance is an example of an organization focused on encouraging correct player, parent, and coach behaviors for a positive youth sports experience.[22]

Mom involvement in coaching is observable at the elementary school level. In the AYSO, for example, the most likely age groups for mom coaching involvement are age groups that include under six (U6), under eight (U8), and under ten (U10). From drills and exercises that develop skills and are fun, to equipment that works well, to game strategy, "Coach Mom" seeks information and appreciates brands that support her. According to Dr. Martha Ewing of the Michigan State University Institute for the Study of Youth Sports, as many as one-third of coaches of female teams are female. Ewing reports that there are several barriers that prevent more moms from coaching, including family time pressures, an expectation that coaches are men, and women's lack of confidence in their coaching skills and expertise.[23] Brands that encourage moms to coach and support them in this role are appreciated.

At a broader level during the middle school years, all moms are "Coach Mom" to a certain extent, though organizations like the Positive Coaching Alliance do suggest role clarity and ask that mom avoid coaching from the sidelines to focus instead on reinforcing her child's effort and good sportsmanship values.

From a marketing standpoint, the elementary school years offer a rich opportunity for brands to tap into athletics as a high-involvement area and "sporty" family lifestyle. For some brands, their product will actually be used or consumed by the elementary schoolchild and/or the child's mom, and so the opportunity to market to the sports mindset is clear. For example, the traditional Wheaties marketing approach encouraged young athletes to eat Wheaties on a game day in order to perform. This approach spoke to both the young athlete and the mom, who have a common interest in good nutrition to support sports performance. The potential for a child's picture to be on the box of Wheaties also held appeal to both mom and child. This box portrait became so ingrained in American culture that sports photography packages commonly offer the child's picture on a Wheaties box as an option along with a team picture, individual photos, and other keepsake items. Today, Wheaties marketing and branding has gone well beyond this approach and the younger child age range, with a high-performance line for serious athletes called "Wheaties Fuel." And the brand continues to affiliate with top athletes. For example, for the Winter 2010 Olympics, the athletes selected for Wheaties box recognition were medalists Shaun White, Lindsey Vonn, and Seth Wescott.[24]

Products and services that address the parent's desire for personalization of their child's picture and/or video within a sporty context hold considerable appeal. They speak to the sports-centered family lifestyle that, for many, dominates the elementary school years. For other brands and organizations, there is an opportunity to tap into this family lifestyle through partnerships and creative approaches. For example, providing team jerseys, water bottles, or sports towels with branded logos from the sponsoring organization is a time-tested approach to addressing this group.

As we have seen, for moms, the elementary school years have a heavy emphasis on sports participation for the children (and hence the family), rather than emphasizing general exercise and fitness. For mom, her own personal fitness continues to be a consideration, but the sports-centered family lifestyle is more top-of-mind for mom as it involves the whole family. As an alternative to organized sports for brands with a focus on exercise, an activity that becomes most popular among both children and their moms in elementary school years is bike riding, and 52 percent of moms of elementary schoolchildren report their child bikes at least once a week.[25] Biking can be explored as an individual leisure and fitness activity, family activity together, or from a safety angle (e.g., bicycle safety days).

Middle Schoolers

With the move into middle school, the child's own preferences and aptitudes for extracurricular activities are often more defined than they were at the earlier ages. Some middle schoolchildren already have a favorite sport and will spend more time engaged in that focus. In this situation, the most comfortable, familiar path for the mom is to leverage the knowledge and the network that she has already built up in the child's preferred sport. For instance, if mom has a network of other moms with children in baseball that she feels comfortable with, she can easily do more carpooling and impromptu play dates (e.g., after a practice) with this group as their schedules align more easily. In the case where there are multiple children at home, we have observed some moms who prefer for all of their children to participate in the same sports program. This is typically driven by the oldest child's selection, and there are many practical reasons for this preference. The following example from Angela illustrates this point. Angela's family life revolves around swimming practice four days a week during the week, plus swim meets on weekends.

> Both of my girls (ages eleven and twelve) really like swimming and have been doing this since age four. We drive forty-five minutes each way to get to this high school because the coaches are better than the ones downtown. At this point, I have my son, Mikey (age eight), swim, too, because it just makes sense for the family. For him, it's just good exercise. I don't think he'll ever be as serious about swimming as the girls. Once we finish practice at 7:00 p.m., we drive home, have a quick dinner, and they do their homework. I'm the vice president of the Swimming Club because it just makes sense with as much time as I spend at the pool with the kids.

> ~ Angela, mom of two middle schoolers and an elementary schoolchild

However, it is also common for the middle schoolchild's sports preference to change. Often, both mom and her middle schoolchild want to experiment. This change makes it more challenging for mom to support the child's new interests as a priority in the life of the entire family. In this situation, mom may choose to rely more on the school as the organizing element, so that her middle schoolchild stays after school to participate in an organized school sports activity.

In middle school, peer influence strengthens, and children's friends can have an impact on the preferred extracurriculars. The child may want to participate in more activities than is physically possible. Given the time commitment that many of these activities require, some parents will set a rule of no more than one or two sports, or two or three extracurriculars total. The majority (64 percent) of moms of kids ages seven to twelve report that their child is doing one or two extracurricular activities.[26] Even in a household with only one child and two willing parents, the scheduling logistics can become overwhelming if a sport has two or three practices a week plus games in addition to other extracurriculars like music or scouting. Mom begins to notice that she is spending most of her time driving to these activities. At the same time, her ability to contribute directly in the activity is often reduced. For some moms at this age of child, her role becomes limited to that of the "chauffer."

> Ronnie added basketball during elementary school because one of his best friends suggested it. He ended up really liking basketball and went on to play it in high school. He continued with his music, scouting, and baseball throughout middle school. And at his particular middle school,

which was academically competitive, the sports helped him carve out a niche for self-confidence since he was not the highest achieving student in academics. At one point, though, it got to be too much, too many things. I thought to myself, "He doesn't need all this," and we've got to make choices here. It was a parental epiphany that I was spending all my time driving, and I couldn't even remember the schedule beyond the next day. Up to that point, I wanted to give my son exposure to activities my husband or I had tried and also a wide variety of other activities to see what took. But, at middle school, we needed more focus.

~ Sarah, mom of young adult (reflecting on middle school years)

A brand that encourages school-age children to be active and to participate in sports is Frosted Flakes, as we will see from the case example.

In the middle school years in sports, mom may be less likely than she was in the elementary school years to be the coach or leader. There is also a group of moms whose children stop participating in sports at the middle school age range. In this case, mom may want to reinforce a healthy exercise regimen for her child, as Mickey's comments illustrate:

My main goal is for him to figure out something he enjoys doing that he can maintain. I don't care if he is on a team. The main thing for exercise is that they find something that they enjoy enough to be motivated to do as an adult on their own so they can maintain a healthy lifestyle.

~ Mickey, mom of middle schooler

There is an opportunity for brands and marketers to think about how to connect with mom in the exercise and fitness area, and support her goals at the middle school age range. One example would be for a brand to form a marketing partnership with the Positive Coaching Alliance. Separately, there is also an opportunity to reach out to the moms who remain highly involved in their children's sports activities; these women often hold leadership positions in local clubs and are likely opinion leaders.

Teenagers

By the time her child enters high school, mom's concerns and focus has shifted dramatically from earlier years. While most moms still attend some of their child's extracurriculars (87 percent), mom's attendance at extracurriculars drops from the elementary school peak.[27] Additionally, moms leave the choice of activities more in the hands of their teenage son or daughter,

Frosted Flakes

CASE STUDY

Kellogg's Frosted Flakes undertakes a series of programs and initiatives to advocate physical activity and sports participation for children. For example, the Frosted Flakes "We Are Tigers" commercials show children practicing sports, including soccer, football, and baseball. These commercials include images of a running Tony the Tiger animated mascot, along with active child and teen athletes.[28]

As of 2010, Frosted Flakes offered Youth Achievement Awards, celebrating young athletes in several sports.[29] These awards are the latest example of a multiyear program of Frosted Flakes' support for youth sports. In 2008, Frosted Flakes started the "Earn Your Stripes" program. The program's goals were for children "to believe in themselves to overcome challenges, accomplish their goals and be their very best." The "Earn Your Stripes" program was created in partnership with the AYSO, Little League International, and Girls on the Run International.[30]

Another example of Frosted Flakes' support for youth sports was in 2009, when Frosted Flakes announced a promotion that included plans to renovate fifty local sports fields. This promotion was supported by a Super Bowl advertisement with a national call to action. As Kimberly Miller, vice president of marketing for the Morning Foods Division of the Kellogg Company, says in the press release, "The Super Bowl provides the perfect opportunity for us to launch this Earn Your Stripes initiative as we continue to encourage kids to be more active, eat right and to work hard to achieve their goals."[31]

In summary, the Frosted Flakes brand encourages children to be active through a variety of programs and by showing its branded character, Tony the Tiger, as an energetic supporter of youth fitness and sports.

as Nicole's illustrates below. Her story also depicts a trend we have observed broadly among both moms of young adults and teenagers. In this situation, mom will complete the initial research to support her child's interest without her necessarily having expertise or prior personal knowledge of the subject. Mom's research usually is welcomed, and the teen or young adult views it as helpful input for the his or her own decision making.

Ever since I was little, my mom was the one who drove me to dance classes and took me to get my right stuff, and put my hair up, for ballet. She was always there for me. But when I went into high school, I decided to try different types of dance even though my mom always chose ballet. I was doing more modern and interpretive styles. So my mom helped me by trying to learn about that and even helped me with my ideas on choreography.

~ Nicole, young adult

While moms of teens continue to rate their child's sport program as a high priority, along with physical fitness and exercise, there are fewer opportunities for the mom to participate, even as "chauffer," ferrying her child to and from events. For a mom whose teen can drive, her time commitment for her teen child's sports is more limited than during the elementary school years.

While mom's time commitment in driving to and from games and practices may be reduced in some instances, her purchasing power can still be sought for more specialized equipment and brands that make it easy for mom to support her teen athlete financially, as we will see with the NikeiD case example.

Many sports, fitness, and activity-oriented brands and marketing programs focus directly on the teen athlete as the teens are considered the primary decision maker. NikeiD is an example of this approach that also provides a Web site, making it easy for mom to support her teen athlete's choices.

The approach of marketing directly to the teen with mom as a "purchasing agent" is often appropriate; however, it is worth considering if there are other opportunities for brands interested in connecting with moms of teens. For instance, there are Web sites that give mom and her teen child information about how to get her teenage child scouted for a possible college program.[34] College sports scholarship is an area where focusing on the moms can make sense as there are considerable costs, organizational skills, and time investments required. Another potential opportunity in the exercise and sports area would be for a brand to sponsor mother-daughter programs like exercise classes, gym memberships, or walking clubs.

Young Adults

During the young adult years, mom remains concerned with making sure that her child is active, fit, and healthy. However, mom has a more limited ability to influence this directly. Typically, mom serves as resource for her

NikeiD

The Nike brand successfully delivers the benefit of performance along with the excitement of customization through its NikeiD offering. NikeiD allows an athlete the ability to design the shoe that fits his or her needs and desired image. The service promises personalization. This personalization is accomplished through a choice of independent sizing for right and left shoes, a choice of shoe width, a choice of colors, and the addition of a Personalized iD (PiD). The PiD is a combination of letters, spaces, and numbers that the customer selects.[32]

This approach appeals directly to the athlete, but as we can see from Karly's story below, the NikeiD service also appeals to moms:

> Nike has put out a site where you can customize a football shoe now—wide, extra wide, both physical appearance and internal structure. Tanner pointed it out. And we used the site together to order a shoe. . . . When I saw the Nike Web site, I thought, "It's about time." It's a great marketing tool. It's a no-brainer.

> *~ Karly, mom of two teenagers*

The Nike brand approach of appealing to moms can still be improved upon, however. For example, in April and May of 2010, Nike received negative feedback from moms for the company's continued support of Tiger Woods and Ben Roethlisberger, given these Nike-sponsored athletes' recent questionable personal actions. One blogger mom of young girls called for a boycott and asked that Nike do more to promote girls' sports.[33]

Despite this controversy, NikeiD remains a powerful tool that appeals to young adult athletes and also delivers convenience to the moms of these athletes, through the benefits of customization and personalization.

young adult child, often on an "on-call" basis when the need arises. A mom of a young adult may be asked for advice on a wide range of topics including fashion, food, parenting, gardening, financial products, and other areas. Mom's advice is typically sought out most intensely when the young adult child first experiences a new life situation, but mom's advice is still solicited even after her child gains comfort and experience. In some cases, the mom can provide both general advice as well as more direct support, as Isabel's story illustrates. Isabel stepped in to babysit her daughter's children in order to give her child the time to work out in the gym.

> My daughter, Christy, was active with her two young kids (ages two and three). She was working out and had a gym membership. I would watch the kids so she could work out. For my sons, I talk to them and tell them it's important to get moving around. . . . I have told them over the years, you aren't that tall, so you need to move to get your weight down.
>
> *~ Isabel, mom of young adults*

Because she knows her young adult child well, mom is in a good position to suggest to him or her types of enjoyable exercise and fitness programs based on a deep knowledge of her child's preferences. The young adult children typically are willing to consider mom's advice as it is tailored to them and clearly has their interests at heart. This can be particularly helpful if the child is transitioning from being extremely active in high school to a less active phase in college or adult working life after high school, as Nicole's story illustrates.

> I was dancing twelve-plus hours a week in high school, and that's how I got my exercise. Right after high school, I did nothing, and then nothing in college. Mom said just go out and ride your bike or power walk—she is a big advocate of power walking because she can't run due to arthritis. My mom knows I'm not going to the gym and lift weights for three hours, so when I was at college, she sent me a yoga video. She knows what I like to do, and what I'll be motivated to do. Now that I'm home for the summer, we go (together) on long walks.
>
> *~ Nicole, young adult*

Another example is how Alicia supported her daughter's decision to start a Praise Dance Team at her college. In addition to the transfer of religious values, the activity also provided exercise.

While I would like exercise to be a priority in their life, I want Christ to be at the forefront. If you have God in your life, you will exercise. I was excited because my daughter started the Praise Dance Team (at college). And she called me and wanted a script. It brought to mind that what you taught them they will keep through life. I was hollering and screaming (with joy).

~ Alicia, mom of a young adult

Young adults reach out to mom using cell phone calls, texting, Facebook, and Skype, among other approaches. This presents a marketing opportunity to reach the moms with relevant messages about exercise and fitness that then can be forwarded on by mom to her young adult child. In some cases, it may be easier to reach mom with these messages than the young adult. At this point, many young adult children have moved past the rebellion of their teenage years, and they seek mom's input on a wide range of topics. There can also be opportunities for creative approaches; for instance, a lawn and garden brand like Scotts could deliver a message on the amount of exercise one gets from typical gardening, and how gardening is good exercise in addition to being a rewarding activity in and of itself. Young adults we spoke to mentioned that they do solicit their parents' advice about gardening.

During their child's young adult years, moms often increase their own exercise commitment for health and weight reasons. As examples, moms of young adults mentioned taking walks on breaks at work, walking after getting home from work, gardening to keep fit, and using Nintendo's Wii Fit. When possible from a lifestyle standpoint, mom will invite her young adult child to be her exercise buddy. The roles also can be reversed where the young adult encourages the mom to exercise as well. This presents an opportunity for an organization, product, or service to support young adult and mom together in reaching their exercise goals. Exercise is an important area of mom's focus. Obesity and overweight concerns for her child are common, and are shared by 57 percent of moms in the teen years.[35]

Conclusion

The area of exercise, fitness, and sports holds rich potential for brands and organizations that market to moms. To begin with, moms view fitness and exercise as important to their child's well-being and health. In addition, having her child participate in sports offers mom a natural mechanism for imparting life lessons to the child. Sports can provide lessons in areas like teamwork, good sportsmanship, discipline, practice, and self-control, along with good fun. Some moms take this a step further with greater involvement as the team organizer, or even take on a coaching role. In these sports-oriented roles, mom is actively participating in her child's development in a different way than a traditional caregiving approach. In some families, particularly those with elementary schoolchildren, attending their children's sporting events becomes the dominant family lifestyle on weekends. Shared sports and exercise activities like biking also offer a family activity that all can enjoy, from preschoolers to teens and young adults.

Depending on the age of the child and the intensity of participation, the focus changes for mom. For moms of infants/toddlers, the primary focus is around physical activity and exercise for her child (and herself), much more so than sports. In the preschool years, sports and fitness activities are often selected that mirror the parents' interests and that are convenient for the family lifestyle ("imitation"). In the elementary school years, a wide array of choices open up, and the focus is generally more on sports for the child than fitness ("involved"). In addition, the oldest child's sports interest may tend to set a pattern for younger siblings. In the middle school and high school years, sports choices are made more by the child, and mom's involvement generally decreases ("purchasing agent and driver"). For her young adult children, mom's focus returns to the area of physical fitness and exercise similar to the infant/toddler time frame, and mom takes on a role of "advice giver."

The Theme Resource Guide: Exercise and Sports figure shows how these areas vary by age of child and also by mom's focus when thinking of her child for exercise and sports, as compared with when mom is thinking of her own exercise and sports considerations. For example, when mom's focus is on her child, the peak years for sports participation and importance to mom are when her child is in elementary or middle school. For some moms this involvement with her child's sports extends into high school. Brands that tie in with the child's sports participation will likely want to consider the elementary school age range opportunity first, followed by the middle school and high school options. By comparison, when focused on herself the mom of an infant/toddler will be concerned with getting back in shape. The LUNA Moms Club's partnership with Stroller Strides is a good example of a brand that is meeting the needs of this age group.

Exercise and Sports

THEME RESOURCE GUIDE

	Mom's Concern For Her Child	Mom's Concern For Herself
Infant/Toddler Moms	• Sports not a focus • Exercise by moving around	• Exercise • Get back in shape
Preschool Moms	• Keeping kid active • Sports starting	• Exercise and fitness
Elementary School Moms	• Sports participation family lifestyle	• Exercise and fitness
Middle School Moms	• Sports focus	• Exercise and fitness • Weight management
Moms of Teens	• Depends on whether child plays sports	• Exercise for health
Moms of Young Adults	• More concerns with adult child's exercise but little ability to impact	• Exercise for health

■ = Higher Mom's priority
▨ = Moderate Mom's priority
□ = Lower Mom's priority

There are several examples of brands that have successfully tailored their marketing approaches to address mom's interest and commitment to sports and exercise. These brands recognize how mom's focus adapts by age of child. They range from LUNA's sponsorship of the company's Moms Club, powered by Stroller Strides, to Frosted Flakes' advocacy for sports participation and physical activity, to Nike's success with NikeiD in convincing mom to buy the products for her children who are high school athletes. There is also an opportunity to support moms of young adults in their desire to encourage their adult children to maintain active lives with adequate exercise, perhaps using approaches that leverage the technologies these moms are employing to communicate with their adult children.

In summary, the sports and exercise area is rich with opportunities to reach mom and support her priority of keeping her children active and fit.

Notes

1. Marketing to Moms Coalition, *State of the American Mom* 2009.
2. Ibid., 2007.
3. Ibid.
4. Ibid.
5. Marketing to Moms Coalition, *State of the American Mom* 2007.
6. Ibid., 2009.
7. "5-in-1 Adjustable Gym," accessed May 21, 2011, http://www.amazon.com/5-In-1-Adjustable-Gym/dp/B00079RC5K/ref=sr_1_2?ie=UTF8&s=baby-products&qid=1306003048&sr=8-2.
8. Marketing to Moms Coalition, *State of American Mom* 2010.
9. "Stroller Strides FAQ's," accessed May 21, 2011, http://www.strollerstrides.com/programs-locations/stroller-strides-faqs.
10. Luna Mom's Club, accessed May 21, 1011, http://www.strollerstrides.com/programs-locations/luna-moms-club.
11. Marketing to Moms Coalition, *State of the American Mom* 2010.
12. "Signature 3: Get Your Kids Started Early with Our Kids Signature Programs," accessed May 21, 2011, http://www.parkcitymountain.com/winter/school/kids_signature_programs/signature-3/index.html.
13. "Our Story," accessed May 21, 2011, http://www.lunabar.com/story/company/.
14. "Moms with a Mission," accessed May 21, 2011, http://www.lunabar.com/life/luna_moms_club/.

15. "To Mama Flora," "Come Together" section of Luna Web site, accessed May 21, 2011, http://lunabar.com/S=94cb375a093d7e9c2aeb20cbdfeea 672fdfc6d85/life/inspiration/P20/.

16. Marketing to Moms Coalition, *State of the American Mom* 2010.

17. Redmon Fun and Fitness Exercise Equipment for Kids—Tread Mill," accessed May 21, 2011, http://www.amazon.com/Redmon-Fitness-Exercise-Equipment-Kids/dp/B00139YBQQ/ref=acc_glance_ba_ai_ps_t_1.

18. "Infant & Toddler—Baby Chair/Camp Chair," accessed May 21, 2011, http://www.redmonusa.com/Results.cfm?category=5&secondary=27.

19. "Child Care," accessed May 21, 2011, http://clubs.lifetimefitness.com/Family-Child-Center/16304/.

20. Marketing to Moms Coalition, *State of the American Mom* 2007.

21. Ibid.

22. "Second-Goal Parent: Developing Winners in Life Through Sports," accessed May 21, 2011, http://shopping.positivecoach.org/Courses/Second-Goal-Parent.

23. Personal interview with Dr. Martha Ewing of the Michigan State University Institute for the Study of Youth Sports on May 25, 2010.

24. "Shaun White, Lindsey Vonn, and Seth Wescott Celebrate Golden Achievements With a Wheaties Win: America's Star Winter Athletes Grace Special-Edition Wheaties Packages," March 4, 2010, accessed May 21, 2011, http://www.generalmills.com/en/Media/NewsReleases/Library/2010/March/Golden_Achievments_With_Wheaties_Win.aspx.

25. Marketing to Moms Coalition, *State of the American Mom* 2010.

26. Ibid., 2007.

27. Marketing to Moms Coalition, *State of the American Mom* 2007.

28. "Frosted Flakes We are Tigers Commercial.mpg," accessed May 21, 2011, http://www.youtube.com/watch?v=kAIIb2j-xVw.

29. "Youth Achievement: About YAA," accessed May 21, 2011, http://www.frostedflakes.com/About-YAA.aspx.

30. "Kellogg's Frosted Flakes Gold Helps Mom Get the Gold," February 4, 2008, accessed May 21, 2011, http://www.smartbrief.com/news/fmi/industryPR-detail.jsp?id=04AFEA27-5DAB-4AFC-9009-D33E678C2594.

31. "Kellogg's Frosted Flakes Cereal to Announce National Field Renovation Program to Millions of Families During Super Bowl Ad," January 27, 2009, accessed May 21, 2011, http://kelloggs.mediaroom.com/index.php?s=43&item=237.

32. "What is NIKEiD?," accessed May 21, 2011, http://help-us.nike.com/app/answers/detail/a_id/3392/~/what-is-nikeid%3F.

33. "Why Moms Should Boycott Nike," accessed May 21, 2011, www.blogher.com/why-moms-should-boycott-nike.

34. "Home," accessed May 22, 2011, http://www.college-athletic-scholarships.com/.

35. Marketing to Moms Coalition, *State of the American Mom* 2010.

CHAPTER 4

Education: From LeapFrog to College

Often, long before a child is born, the parents have begun planning his or her future. A large part of this planning involves education—learning, some say, begins before birth when the baby is still in the womb; mom and dad talk to, sing to, and play language tapes to the unborn child. In competitive urban areas, the enrollment process for preschool programs often begins before birth.

Across all income levels, whether mom has one child or many, infant or teen, the quality of the child's education ranks as a very high priority for mom, third only to her relationship with the child and the quality of communication between them.[1] Education is such a high priority that while other purchases may be deferred in times of economic hardship, education is relatively recession-proof. In 2009, when many families struggled financially, some 54 percent of all moms still planned to spend on education for their children or themselves. This contrasts with the 39 percent of moms who planned to buy a major home appliance in the same year.[2] The same priority for education was also seen in 2010, with 50 percent of moms planning to spend on education as compared with 34 percent who planned to buy a major appliance.[3] Education was far ahead of a new home, a new car, and appliance purchases.[4] Moms with children ages thirteen to seventeen were the most likely group to continue to direct their resources to education, with 68 percent of moms in this age group going ahead with planned educational spending despite the recession.[5] Among moms of infants and toddlers, who have little time, nearly 50 percent still made education a spending priority.[6]

Infants/Toddlers

Once a baby is born, formal education soon comes into focus. The form this education takes varies according to financial means, but a shared goal of moms of infants and toddlers is stimulation and socialization for their babies. Zola's comment vividly illustrates this objective:

> Mostly, right now I'm concerned with social interaction. It is something they have to learn, because she is an only child and all of her cousins are older than her. We try to go to the library and interact with kids there.

~ Zola, mom of an infant/toddler

Toys and games that aid child development are top-selling; moms often are willing to pay the price that comes with such products. Trusted names and developmental toys fare especially well. Johnson & Johnson's Red Rings came to mind for Kansas mother Sarah, whose son is now grown:

> I remember those toys. In fact, I still have some of them because they were so classic. I felt like they had been tested from a developmental perspective to help children's physical coordination and brain development, and the name Johnson & Johnson is such a huge, well-known, and reliable [name].

~ Sarah, mom of a young adult (reflecting on infant/toddler years)

Sarah notes that the quality of the toy became increasingly important as her son moved from infancy to toddler to preschooler and into the realm of imaginative play. "In the toddler years, the choice of toys became even more important. We really pushed those that were developmentally appropriate, but the toys became even more important as he got older," she said. Discovery Toys, which are sold by mail or through day care centers, were among her favorite. "We still have some of them, because they were really high quality toys," Sarah continued. "They were offered in the child care center for sale, and you could go in and look at them in that setting where you trusted they would take care of your child."

Formal education, which once began in elementary school, now starts as early as age three or four, when parents enroll their children in toddler programs a few days a week for a few hours at a time. The national average for school enrollment for three- and four-year-olds was 53 percent in 2008.[7] This includes any type of graded public, parochial, or other private school, including nursery schools and kindergartens. It is interesting to note that this enrollment level roughly approximates the percentage of preschool

FIGURE 4.1. PERCENTAGE OF THE POPULATION AGES THREE TO FOUR ENROLLED 1994-2008

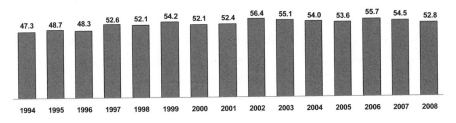

Source: U.S. Department of Commerce, Census Bureau, *Current Population Survey (CPS)*, October Supplement, 1994-2008

moms who work.[8] Some private schools have recognized this very early childhood market (prior to preschool), and they have chosen to offer toddler and mother/toddler programs with the hope of capturing future students for their preschool and elementary programs.

Moms who choose preschool and toddler educational programs hope for an experience that will deliver early education. These programs are an important way to meet the needs of young families, and they also offer a way for brands to reach mom when she is thinking about her child's education at this very early inflection point.

Moms of infants and toddlers identify ample opportunity for learning outside of the classroom, whether with toys or educational video games and television programs. From a very early age now, children are using computer games and scrolling across iPhone screens using apps designed especially for them. Moms across all income levels are interested in engaging with their children in activities that promote brain development, and they are often willing to pay more for such products, many of which are electronic.

Julie, whose son is two, has a tech-savvy toddler. He speaks to his father, who is deployed in the military, via Skype. He knows his way around an iPhone and can get in and out of toddler games. He visits the *Sesame Street* Web site online, though he hasn't quite mastered the keyboard. Another mom, Zola, notes that her two-year-old daughter uses the iPhone's coloring application.

Educational television also plays an important role, with the educational television classic *Sesame Street* a perennial favorite among moms we interviewed. A variety of other programs also capture this audience. Mom Zola raves about the PBS program *WordWorld*. Another program mentioned by Yolanda, a single mother, is Nickelodeon's *Noggin*. Along with the programs come related Web sites, toys, DVDs, and other merchandise that is popular with moms of children in this age group.

Brands that can connect with a child through one medium—like TV or other technology—have a ready opportunity to create line extensions, bringing their characters to life through stuffed animals and dolls, like Elmo and SpongeBob. And brands that support the mom of an infant or toddler in her role as her child's first teacher are appreciated, particularly by first-time moms.

Preschoolers

Among moms of preschoolers, we noted similar needs in the area of education to those of moms with infants/toddlers. Moms continue to be concerned with socialization, as underscored by Bonita's comments:

> Academically, I don't have any goals for her yet. Instead, my goal is for her to be social. She doesn't have any siblings, and I didn't want her at home not socializing with anyone. This is important, because when she does enter kindergarten, she can get along with others and share.

> ~ Bonita, mom of preschooler

Bonita was also one mother among many who expressed a desire for her child to love reading. She cites Dr. Seuss books as a popular brand. Familiar to many generations, Dr. Seuss (published by Random House) has now created an online community, Seussville, complete with a newsletter ("Seussville News"), online activities (e.g., *One Fish Two Fish* Concentration), and events, including Read Across America.[9]

Another brand that has leveraged multiple channels is the interactive product LeapFrog, a favorite of moms and children in this age group. The case study illustrates why.

Elementary Schoolchildren

The academic and social quality of a child's education becomes—and will remain—an important focus for mom in the elementary school years. Moms in all income groups will fight hard for a quality education and will find ways to put their children in the best schools. This may mean making sacrifices in other areas.

LeapFrog

LeapFrog is a developer of innovative technology-based educational products. The company is "100 percent focused on developing products that will provide the most engaging, effective learning experience—for all ages, in school or home, around the world. We put learning first—a philosophy that distinguishes us from our competitors and fuels the entire company."[10] This philosophy resonates with moms. "We like the LeapFrog Learning stuff for all the kids. All of the kids have used it," said Mickey, a fitness instructor with boys ages one, two, eight, and eleven.

One of the company's recent creations, the Leapster Explorer, leverages kids' interest in technology and penchant for handheld devices. The Explorer includes Flash and 3-D graphics, and the product supports downloadable applications like videos and e-books, as well as a camera accessory. The Explorer enables users to access programs online through LeapWorld. One application allows children the opportunity to create a pet, then take the pet with them online into Leap-World and back to the Explorer, earning treats and accessories for their pet along the way.[11]

Like most of the LeapFrog materials, the Explorer stores information about a child's progress and adjusts game and activity challenges in real time. Mom can monitor her child's progress through the Leap-Frog Learning Path. As stated by Craig Hendrickson, senior vice president and chief product officer, in a press release from June 7, 2010:

> We know that children are just as interested in today's hottest technologies as their parents are, so we are particularly excited to introduce Leapster Explorer, which combines cutting-edge capabilities like finger-touch and downloadable apps with solid educational content and kid-friendly durability. Add the online LeapWorld for kids and Learning Path for parents, and you have a breakthrough device that supports an incredible variety of ways to learn and play, all at a price that parents will like.[12]

LeapFrog also provides a variety of online resources for mom—from an FAQ section to learning tips to "quick printables," which are activi-

LeapFrog (continued)

ties sheets that mom can quickly download and use with her child. A rich community section allows mom to connect with other moms, as well as LeapFrog experts like kindergarten teacher Shelby Moore, who contributes to the LeapFrog blog with such posts as "What can you do this summer to prepare your child for next year?" An on-staff literacy expert also shares tips and resources with parents, offering such practical advice as "Hunt for letters and words wherever you are" and "go on a rhyming treasure hunt."[13] Thus, LeapFrog's products appeal to moms' desire to give their children a head start.

"I think that education is one of the most important things I can do for him, and I can't do much else for him right now," said Yolanda, a single mother whose son, age seven, is in first grade. Dissatisfied with the quality of the local public schools, she applied for and was granted a scholarship to a parochial school. "It was the best thing I ever did for him," she said. "They keep him so stimulated. I want to make sure he gets a solid foundation early on that he can take anywhere."

Moms of elementary schoolchildren have opportunities to be directly engaged in the educational experience in many schools as room mothers, field trip chaperones, fund-raisers, lunchroom workers, Parent-Teacher Association (PTA) members, and more. Schools and teachers are generally happy to accept mom's help as an extra set of hands for fund-raising, running events, and other administrative activities. However, they are generally less interested in mom's help or contribution in the area of curriculum or classroom practices. The mindset is that the important core area of the teaching should be the realm of trained experts. This can create a situation where sports programs are more open to mom (i.e., she can watch her child practice and play sports and even coach) than her child's classroom. The classroom may be open on selected occasions or for certain activities (e.g., a classroom book reading or parent's night), but generally it is closed. Regardless of the rationale, this ultimately means that mom has less access to the classroom than she does to the sports field. As a result, the child is more likely to see mom at his or her sporting events and practices, and this more visible parent involvement in sports can lead to an unintended message that sports are more important to the mom than her child's education. Sarah's story illustrates this:

> With my background in teaching English part time to non-native English speakers as well as my time in high school administration, I felt well-qualified to assist in a curricular way in my son Ronnie's school. I negotiated with my employer a schedule that would allow me to leave work early two days a week in order to be in my son's school, and I contacted the teacher to volunteer. My son's teacher said that she couldn't use me in her classroom, but the school could use me to assist with special education. I thought that was a good starting point, so I contacted the special education teacher who told me that the opening would be to assist with the special education group five days a week for two hours a day. I told her I couldn't do that due to working full time. The school then suggested I work in the library returning books to their shelves. I declined. It just wasn't possible, even with my background, to be in the school in a meaningful way. In contrast, I was able to be the scorekeeper for my son's baseball team and help out. I couldn't coach, not being a baseball player, but I could play a meaningful role that helped the other parents who were coaching and got me involved in the game. I would consider myself a big "education first" person, but the school opportunities just weren't open in the way that sports were.

> ~ *Sarah, mom of a young adult (reflecting on elementary school)*

Educational television and computer programs continue to play an influential role in the development of elementary schoolchildren and as a valued resource for mom. Yolanda attributes her son's interest in karate to a television. She credits another show with stimulating her son's imagination, as well as teaching him manners. Another mom, Corkey, praises Hooked on Phonics, which her mother purchased for her son. Corkey believes Hooked on Phonics provides her son with an advantage in school.

Helping mom provide her child with additional learning opportunities, whether it be access to better education, educational resources, or specific tools or programs, will garner her loyalty. Brands that connect with mom in the educational area can form a powerful bond.

Middle Schoolers

Middle school takes curriculum and homework to a new level for moms and their children. Middle school students take classes from several subject matter expert teachers instead of a single teacher. With this change, it becomes more difficult for mom to engage in a child's daily education. For many moms, volunteer activities in the school and contact with teachers may decrease during the middle school years. As a result, the greatest exposure to a child's school day may come through homework.

Another shift is that mom now begins to get more focused on her child's achievement and continuing character development during the often tumultuous junior high years. In addition to the importance of quality classroom experiences, mentors including Scout leaders and athletic coaches play a significant role.

> School achievement and then character development was really important to me in the tween years. At that point in time, kids seem to start to run into kids who have some really different value systems. They're getting much more aware of the outside world and differences, and that's when I think you have a lot of talking to do with them about why people are different and our family holds the values we hold.

> ~ *Sarah, mom of a young adult (reflecting on middle school years)*

While she helps supervise homework during the child's middle school years, mom also tries to help the child build a habit of self-reliance and autonomy. Thus, she not only assists with keeping track of assignments, but she also helps the child problem-solve in ways that will ensure greater independence once the child moves into high school.

A favorite tool that these moms rely on is the Internet; fully one-third of moms are using the Internet to help their middle schoolchildren with homework. This reflects a significant increase from elementary school levels.[14]

Many schools and teachers use the Internet as a way to communicate with parents. Schools use e-mail and their own Web sites to provide announcements and news and to deliver forms like field trip permission slips. Teachers may use school Web sites to post assignments and worksheets. This creates an opportunity for a brand to sponsor a homework club—either locally through community stores and/or distributors or online. In the same way that Tony the Tiger and the Frosted Flakes brand are encouraging children to be active and participate in fitness and sports activities, a brand can encourage kids to do their homework. There is also the opportunity for a brand to connect with a specific topic, such as science or a foreign language. Based on mom's use of the Internet for homework, we believe that mom will appreciate brands that can help her access specialized resources that are helpful for her child's education. For example, there are Web sites that offer online games to help reinforce vocabulary in foreign languages. Providing links or special content offers and promotions in these forums can help to reinforce mom's desire to promote her child's learning.

Several brands have found novel ways to help mom promote her child's learning, while at the same time providing an enjoyable "assignment," as well as a monetary award. The earned media and goodwill from moms that these brands receive far exceeds the scholarship or prize money awarded. One such example is Olive Garden's Pasta Tales, an essay contest that poses a different question every year. The 2010 question: "Describe a teacher who has inspired you in school and tell how he or she has impacted your life." The essays are reviewed by the Quill and Scroll Society of the College of Journalism and Communication at the University of Iowa. Winners receive a $500 savings bond and dinner with their family at their local Olive Garden restaurant. In their news release, Steve Coe, Olive Garden spokesperson, said, "Our goal with Pasta Tales is to spark imagination and provide a platform for individual personalities to shine through."[15]

Similarly, the America & Me Essay Contest was founded by Farm Bureau Insurance in 1968 to encourage Michigan youth to explore their roles in America's future. Since that time, nearly a half-million Michigan eighth graders have participated in the contest. In 2009-2010 over 5,000 students from nearly 500 Michigan junior highs and middle schools participated. The student essays for the contest were based on the topic "My Personal Michigan Hero." Winners receive plaques, medallions, and $1,000.[16]

Such contests, as Melissa notes, nurture critical thinking skills, strengthening the child's academic foundation:

> Early childhood education is all about the fundamentals. Middle school marks the point where we as moms begin to really challenge our kids as independent thinkers. What does the Trail of Tears mean for us as humans? How can we impact our peers to learn from these lessons? Companies that support these deeper levels of understanding and change with unique essay and poetry contests support not only our children, but our individual core beliefs and sense of purpose.
>
> *~ Melissa, mom of a middle schooler*

Teenagers

A college education for her child may well have been an expectation or a hope for mom even long before her baby was conceived. Similarly, a college education for her child holds interest during the elementary and middle school years but is still a fairly distant goal. In her child's high school years, however, college becomes a more serious emphasis for mom. Likewise, postsecondary alternatives to college, such as the military, trade school, and employment begin to loom in the future as options for her child. Education also takes on an additional dimension, as teenage children learn to drive and to take on other forms of independence.

Teenagers do quite a bit of college research on their own, but many moms (and dads) are also fully engaged. Mom can be trusted to do some of the upfront research for her child, as Niki's story about her mom's help with the research for college choices illustrates:

> My mom was extremely involved, did all of the research, and showed me a list. She would set up the visits with the admission office and did her work on that. I have a twin brother so the two of us went through this at the same time, in part for scheduling so no conflict, so it would run smoothly. I was completely happy, she did an amazing job, went above and beyond. During high school she kept me focused so I did not become overly emotional and get into the drama with my friends. She would say education is important, you have to have good grades.
>
> *~ Niki, a young adult*

In our experience, mom is not confined to "desk research" for college and educational choices for her teen. She will also take her child on college visits, attend school presentations with their child, and help her child sort through choices. Visits to college campuses can start as early as sophomore year in high school, or they may begin junior year. By the start of senior year, a group of teenagers and their parents often have a well-defined list of college choices. Similar to the dynamic seen with younger children, many moms will suggest their own college as a choice for their child. This mom recommendation can be a serious influence.

For Sarah, the mother of a son who is now twenty-one, the brand that most resonated during high school years was, interestingly, not a detergent or auto make, but a college brand.

> The branding that became important at this point in time was academic reputation. I know this is why we chose Creighton, because it

had a stellar image. We agreed with its brand image and thought it was a good one that fit with us.

~ Sarah, mom of a young adult

Financial considerations play a defining role in college choices, perhaps even more today than in the past. This means colleges and universities must work even harder to sell themselves, not only to the student, but also to the parent portion of the market. Parents, who are most involved at the beginning and the end of the application process, are especially concerned about career preparation.[17] They want to see a large investment pay off. As Kay Kimball Gruder notes on her college parenting Web site: "With the huge investment that college entails, it is natural to want to ensure your child's success. At the same time, the pre-college and college years are developmentally important for your child to take increased responsibility for decisions, interactions, goals and planning for the future."[18]

It is this "letting go" versus "wanting to know" dynamic that causes parents to report feeling frustrated, worried, anxious, and uncertain about their parenting and their child's success. Gruder's Web site goes on to suggest a series of questions that concerned parents should ask themselves:

- Do you ever feel like you want to help your child, but you just don't know how?

- Do you ever find yourself getting too involved and then kicking yourself afterward?

- Do you wonder what's really going on?

- Do you desire more strategies and tools to assist you in your parenting?

- Do you want a greater understanding of the resources available to your son or daughter at their college?

- Do you want to effectively guide your son or daughter to make the most of opportunities both inside and outside the classroom?[19]

After reviewing the above questions, interested parents can then consider a range of professional services offered by Gruder.

However, it is also important to keep in mind that the definition of her child's education for many moms does not have to include college; it can be an alternative, like a proven trade school. We also found that mom's own personal experience can lead to her commitment to higher education for her child. Several lower-income single moms that we interviewed made it a priority to go to school at night. These moms' expectation is that education will lead to a better job and more opportunities. When considering this expanded definition of education, mom's role is to make sure her child will make an informed choice. For example, several moms of high school teenage girls mentioned that their daughters are considering cosmetology. These moms expressed concerns that they share with their daughters around the business considerations of developing a clientele and the variable paycheck associated with the cosmetology occupational choice.

It can also be difficult for moms to provide direct help to her child in the area of high school homework. So, for example, Eleanor outsources direct contact on the academic front, paying to have a tutor from a local university work with her son and relying on high school teachers as the primary educational resource.

Brands that can provide resources or services that help parents guide their child through the decision-making process for "what's next" after high school will win mom's approval.

Young Adults

Once a child is out of high school and on to college or life's next chapter, mom takes on an important advisory role. Moms with children in college may provide input on class choices, nutrition, social life, fashion, safety, and a host of other issues. In some cases, mom continues to finance education, insurance, clothing, nutrition, and other purchases for her young adult child.

Margarita, a single mother of a nineteen-year-old daughter, houses and insures both her daughter and her daughter's child, paying for her grandson's day care. Moms continue to make sacrifices and influence their young adult child's life choices, with education being a prime example. Yolanda's daughter has considered many programs—from personal training to cosmetology—each eliciting advice from mom, who researches the programs, offers advice on careers, and is fully involved in the process.

> As a mom, I try to convince her she should try to get some degree. First she was going to go into elementary education, but she's changed her

mind. She wants to go to another college and be a personal trainer. I just want her to get something under her belt. From the time she started out, I have always said "go to school, go to school, go to school."

~ Margarita, mom of young adult

On the other end of the spectrum is Eleanor, who has a daughter, age nineteen, and a son, age fifteen. Eleanor works thirty hours a week. Her husband, a professor, works full time. Their children have the benefit of parents who can afford tutors for their high school son and are also able to send their daughter to a private college in the United States as well as to Italy for study-abroad experience. Eleanor's focus is less on her young adult daughter's academic performance. Instead, she focuses on socialization, making the right choices, and driver responsibility for her daughter. Eleanor is confident that her daughter is getting a good education at her music-focused college, and she is concerned more about the other aspects of her daughter's life such as social, physical, and emotional.

Diane, whose children are twenty-one, twenty-five, and thirty-one, views herself as an advisor to her children, who she says consult her frequently. She does not have a college degree and believes she has given them the tools they need to make their own decisions, having reinforced the importance of education throughout their lives. Her twenty-one-year-old daughter initially wanted to become a teacher but since high school has dabbled in beauty school and teaches dance at a local studio. "I told her it was her decision and that she needs to make the right one. I've given you guys all the tools," Diane said.

Diane's older two male children have completed college degrees and are employed—one as the manager of a fitness center and the other in the IT department of the local school district. She is thankful for the guidance of a professor:

> He taught him a lot and taught me so much. He was real hard on the class and on the kids. He was a role model and took my son [who works in IT] under his wing. They knew they needed a college degree. I would do whatever I could and have, financially, in various ways. College degrees are essential, and a trade of some other sort is also essential to go along with that.

~ Diane, mom of three young adults

Sarah, whose son is nearly twenty-two, was involved in his education throughout his childhood, but she says he is establishing his independence and bristles against too much advice.

> School achievement is still a really hot topic because it's such a foundation for later life, but right now he is establishing his independence from me, trying to make all his own decisions and be an adult and not make mistakes—of course you do have to make mistakes—but he is very sensitive to me trying to [make decisions for him].

> *~ Sarah, mom of a young adult*

The military remains an important option for many high school students and their moms, especially if one or both parents took that route and finances are tight. Isabel, age forty-two, has three grown children, all of whom participated in Marine Reserve Officer Training Corp (ROTC) in their high school. Justin, age twenty-three, joined the Marines after high school. Kristin, age twenty-two, was more influenced by a middle school experience as a volunteer working with horses and disabled children. She went on to college to study physical therapy.

> ROTC took up a lot of our time. To be honest, that's what saved them from getting into bad things in high school. They took classes and also did fund-raising and competitions for the drills. It kept them occupied. My main thing, I wanted them to hopefully succeed in life and stay out of trouble.

> *~ Isabel, mom of three young adults*

Conclusion

A number of factors have come together to generate more mom involvement and interest in her children's extracurriculars and education than ever before. While moms are committed to their child's educational quality, their greatest ability to be personally involved in these programs on an ongoing basis tends to be in the elementary and preschool years. In those years, a marketer that speaks to mom's involvement supporting the child will be speaking her language. In contrast, in later middle school and high school years, mom's involvement tends to be more project- or event-focused (e.g., the college choice process, the driver's education process). Additionally, in

Purdue University

Today's parents of young adults are often described as older and better educated than previous generations of parents, increasingly second-generation college graduates, more affluent and media-aware, and very devoted to their child's success. As these parents—often with mom leading the charge—have become increasingly active in their children's activities, even colleges have changed the way they market to dads and moms. Many universities have increased both the volume and nature of communications they share with parents. Purdue University is one such example.

Purdue University's Admissions Office has been distributing parental communications for the past ten years, but the volume (especially with electronic and social media) recently has increased significantly. The residence hall and fund-raising organizations have had parent and family advisory boards since 2004, and both produce either a hard copy or electronic newsletter.

The University increased its distribution of the parent e-newsletter by 94 percent in the 2009-2010 school year, citing 50 percent open rates (which means half of the recipients opened—if not read—the newsletter). Popular topics ranged from the mundane, such as winter weather information, to the nurturing, such as how to order a "Boiler Treat Pack" for one's child.

In addition to the newsletter, there is a University Web site specifically for parents and families (http://www.purdue.edu/purdue/Parents_families/index.html).[20] The site includes archived issues of the electronic newsletter, icons linked to social media options for parents, a rotating photo banner, and a subscription box for the e-newsletter.

The University also hosts a parents and families Facebook page. Conversation threads include how students travel without a vehicle, advisor issues, shuttle services, icy sidewalks, tutoring, Safe Walk escort service, summer internships, and employment.

The University also produces a family calendar. More than a collection of over a dozen beauty shots of campus, the calendar includes a wealth of information designed to provide mom with peace of mind,

Purdue University (continued)

as well as the details she needs to help her child successfully navigate campus life. Its introduction (2010) states:

> With your student newly enrolled at Purdue University. . . you may very well be caught in that tug-of-war between excitement and anxiety. We share your excitement about having a young Boilermaker on the brink of a new life adventure. We understand your anxiety about the year ahead. Please accept this calendar with its Purdue scenes and campus highlights. We present it with the hope that you will use it for tracking important family dates and for the information that we believe will help your family and your student negotiate this year of transition.[21]

Just below the August calendar is a list of "transition tips for parents," including such suggestions as "empower your student to take the initiative and solve his or her own problems" and "send care packages!" Other sections include a "primer on Purdue lingo," "parent involvement opportunities," "roommate conflicts," and the school's fight song.

With these efforts, Purdue University succeeds in recognizing the importance of communicating with mom as well as her young adult college student.[22]

later years, mom will welcome outside expertise from brands that support her general goals and reinforce messages to her children.

Education and extracurricular activities that build character are natural mom preferences and present excellent opportunities for marketers to connect with mom around topics of interest.

Brands like LeapFrog provide moms of younger children with tools to be involved in their child's education, while many universities, such as Purdue, offer regular communication with parents through a variety of mediums to keep mom connected with her child. There are also opportunities for brands to support mom's focus on education with programs for middle school and elementary school students; programs like Olive Garden's Pasta Tales provide monetary incentives and relevant questions to help mom reinforce writing skills and engagement, strengthening the academic foundation she knows is so important to her child's success. The Theme Resource

Education

THEME RESOURCE GUIDE

	Mom's Concern For Her Child	Mom's Concern For Herself
Infant/Toddler Moms	• Gross motor skills and cognitive stimulation	• Some are getting degrees
Preschool Moms	• Gross motor skills and cognitive stimulation • Socialization • Pre-K skills – colors, shapes	• Some are getting degrees
Elementary School Moms	• Adjustment to classroom • Academic building blocks	• Some are getting degrees
Middle School Moms	• Academic foundation • Getting good grades	• Some are getting degrees
Moms of Teens	• Getting good grades • College • Scholarship	• Less involved for self
Moms of Young Adults	• Career/job results from education • Making good choices	• Less involved for self

■ = Higher Mom's priority
▨ = Moderate Mom's priority
□ = Lower Mom's priority

Guide (Mom's Concern for Her Child version) highlights how a mom's focus on the hot-button topic of education shifts over time. For example, the elementary school years emphasize the academic building blocks of reading and writing. By the young adult years, mom's educational focus for her child is more on career, job results, and making good choices.

Another area that may be appealing is for a brand to celebrate moms who have completed their education while being a mom, perhaps through a contest. This type of recognition allows mom to be a role model for her child and reinforces her educational values. The Theme Resource Guide (Mom's Concerns for Herself version) shows that mom as an educational role model is relevant to several age of child groups, particularly infant/toddler, preschooler, elementary schoolchild, and middle schooler.

As the Theme Resource Guide illustrates, many educational aspects are high on mom's priority list and an excellent way to capture her attention.

Notes

1. Marketing to Moms Coalition, *State of the American Mom* 2009.
2. Ibid.
3. Ibid., 2010.
4. Ibid.
5. Ibid., 2009.
6. Ibid.
7. U.S. Department of Commerce, Census Bureau, Current Population Survey (CPS), October Supplement, 1994-2008.
8. Marketing to Moms Coalition, *State of the American Mom* 2010.
9. "Read Across America is Today! This year the NEA's Read Across America Day is being celebrated today, March 2nd, the birthday of Dr. Seuss!," accessed May 15, 2011, http://www.seussville.com/news/seussville_news_march11.html.
10. LeapFrog (n.d.), "About us," accessed July 2, 2010, http://www.leapfrog.com/en/home/about_us.html.
11. LeapFrog (n.d.), "Leapster Explorer," accessed July 2, 2010, http://www.leapfrog.com/explorer/.
12. LeapFrog (June 7, 2010), "LeapFrog Leads the Way in Mobile Learning with New Leapster Explorer Platform," accessed May 15, 2011, http://www.leapfrog.com/en/home/about_us/leapfrog_press_room0/leapster-explorer.html.

13. LeapFrog (March 1, 2010), "Engage Early Readers Through Interactive Learning Experiences," accessed May 15, 2011, http://www.4-traders.com/LFROG-ENTPRS-13383/news/LFROG-ENTPRS-Engage-Early-Readers-Through-Interactive-Learning-Experiences-13333157/.

14. Marketing to Moms Coalition, *State of the American Mom* 2010.

15. English Journal, "Pasta Tales Essay Contest," accessed July 2, 2010, http://www.englishjournal.colostate.edu/Awards/Pasta%20Tales%20Essay%20Contest.htm.

16. Farm Bureau Insurance, "America & Me Essay Contest," accessed May 15, 2011, http://www.farmbureauinsurance-mi.com/pages/america/am-contest.htm.

17. Lipman Hearne, "New Rules in College Choice: Findings from Lipman Hearne's National Study on High-Achieving Seniors," accessed July 2, 2010, http://www.slideshare.net/lipmanhearne/new-rules-in-college-choice-findings-from-lipman-hearnes-national-study-on-highachiev-ing-seniors.

18. Kay Kimball Gruder, (n.d.), "Why Parent Coaching," accessed July 1, 2010, http://www.successfulcollegeparenting.com/WhyParentCoaching.en.html.

19. Ibid.

20. Purdue University, accessed July 1, 2010, www.purdue.edu/purdue/Parents_families/index.html.

21. Purdue University, Family Calendar, 2010-2011.

22. Ibid.

CHAPTER 5

Safety and Health: Safety Gates, Stranger Danger, and Designated Drivers

The physical safety of her children weighs heavily on the mind of mom, rating as one of her most important priorities. Mom knows, both instinctively and intellectually, that her first priority is to keep her child safe and healthy. The only topics considered more important by mom are the quality of communication with her child, her relationship with her child, and the quality of her child's education.[1] As Irma's comments illustrate, physical safety of their child is considered "very important" by 86 percent of moms:

> Health and safety are the most important [priorities for Mom] because if you don't have them, you have nothing and can't enjoy life. I place the top priority on their being safe.

> *~ Irma, mom of a middle schooler, teenager, and young adult*

In addition to physical safety, several other health and safety-related topics are also very important to moms. These include concerns about online safety (i.e., cyber safety), healthy habits, avoiding drug/alcohol use, and safe/responsible driving for teens and young adults.[2]

Moms are highly involved with their child's safety and health at all age ranges, but the emphasis shifts as her child ages. The mom "safety" focus starts before the child is born, and is highlighted immediately after birth, when, for example, mom is instructed to make sure the child car seat is properly installed before leaving the hospital. In contrast, moms of young adults report that they are frequently asked for advice on "health" by their adult children, but are less concerned about their young adult's physical safety.

Daniel, who is twenty-one years old, always asks for my advice. If he is sick, he asks me what to take or what he should do.

~ Irma, mom of a middle schooler, teenager, and young adult

There are several resources that mom relies upon for health and safety information. Her most trusted information sources include: the family (59 percent), pediatrician/health professional (44 percent), friends (47 percent), doctor's office material (29 percent), and Internet searches (22 percent).[3] More specifically, while family is the top information source for parenting, the pediatricians/doctor's office material is the top information source for health and medical information.[4] Moms' use of these information sources has clear implications for marketers.

While it is authoritative, pediatrician advice can also seem less accessible to moms than Internet subject searches and online research, which has become an initial, highly accessible source across many subjects. While the pediatrician is the leading source for health/medical advice, some moms also admitted to feeling uncomfortable "bothering" the pediatrician about every concern they encounter. Many moms are online daily, and if a safety or health question arises, it is easy to do a little online research. Tammy's approach is typical:

Being a new mom, when my son was an infant, I was pretty neurotic. . . . Overall, I use the Internet quite a bit for sources of parenting information. Everything from official Web sites like the Mayo Clinic to mom's message boards at www.mamasource.com. I started using this Web site because when I had my son, I didn't have a lot of friends with kids to turn to, and my own mom doesn't remember all this information. One of the most frustrating things is the different points of view, but I like to see them . . . right now www.mamasource.com gives me the information that I need.

~ Tammy, mom of a preschooler

While moms of younger children have more confidence around the quality of information sources that are readily available to them, this is not necessarily the case for moms of teenagers and young adults. Moms of these older children told us they are not able to rely as much on doctors and pediatricians or online research to effectively address some of their greatest issues around safety and health. Their pressing concerns include safe driving, safe alcohol consumption, avoiding pregnancy or sexual diseases, and having health insurance coverage. Moms of teens and moms of young adults welcome a brand who partners with them in encouraging safe practices and healthy habits for their children. For a brand to be most supportive in this area, it needs to help mom communicate in an age-relevant way with her child.

Infants/Toddlers

For moms of infants/toddlers, health and safety concerns abound. Specific top-of-mind areas of focus for these moms include baby-proofing the home, choice of car seat, baby bottles or other equipment, safe use of home cleaning products, and appropriate use of children's pain and fever relievers (Motrin and Tylenol). There are many choices a mom must make on the "equipment" for her child (e.g., stroller, baby bottle, toys, etc.), and those products' marketing approaches are often extremely overt regarding safety. With the explosion of information at mom's fingertips, there are also frequent "scares"—recalls and changes in the recommended approach for a mom to navigate.

The infant car seat category receives considerable ongoing focus and attention. For moms of infants, the marketing messages are very focused on safety. For example, a mom visiting the EvenFlo Web site (www.evenflo.com) to do some research can visit a specific safety section of the site called "Safety Made Easier."[5] EvenFlo clearly recognizes mom's safety priorities and makes safety information readily accessible about their products. Mom can also look for safety certification from JPMA, the Juvenile Product Manufacturers Association, which requires independent safety testing for products like strollers.[6] The JPMA certifications are updated annually, again suggesting the need for mom to keep abreast of the latest safety developments. As the story below illustrates, moms receive conflicting information on what is considered a "safe" car seat, even from trusted sources like Consumer Reports, and the currency of the information can change dramatically.

> I researched the heck out of the car seat. We wanted one car seat because it went with a stroller. But then I found out through Consumer Reports that the car seat I bought wasn't as safe as another one, so we returned the original one, the stroller, everything, went out, and bought the new car seat. Then a year later, that whole thing came out on the Consumer Reports that they had screwed up the testing. So then mine (the second one) that was top rated fell to the bottom of the list. Then two months later, it reinstated the other way again, that mine was now back at the top. And the car seat, obviously, is super important to me,

so I'll continue to research it. Every time the rankings shift, and everyone only really cares about the car seat rankings. . . . It's hard to know what information to rely upon.

~ Ellen, mom of an infant/toddler

The car seat example also demonstrates how focused moms can be on better, "safer" products for their babies. Another example is in the plastic baby bottle category. A 2007 study released by Environment California called "Toxic Baby Bottles" reported that bisphenol A is released when the most popular plastic baby bottle brands like EvenFlo, Dr. Brown's, Playtex, or Gerber are heated. The study describes bisphenol A as dangerous because "scientists have linked very low doses of bisphenol A exposure to cancers, impaired immune function, early onset of puberty, obesity, diabetes, and hyperactivity, among other problems." [7] These bottles had previously been considered safe, and the finding caught moms by surprise. The story below gives an idea of the challenges one mom faced with the baby bottle scare.

> I spent a lot of time researching the best baby bottles and chose Dr. Brown's. . . it's supposed to reduce gas and prevent colic. I spent a small fortune on Dr. Brown's and was nearly done with bottle-feeding when I started to hear from my friends that these bottles were "poisoning our babies." I heard that the plastic is toxic, that you, number one shouldn't put it in the dishwasher, number two, you shouldn't have any of these that have PCBs. But then I asked my doctor about it, and even two doctors in the same practice said totally different things. A few months later, Toys "R" Us offered a no-questions-asked exchange program, and so I went back and replaced the bottles with Born Free. While it was great that Toys "R" Us did this, the whole thing was very alarming!

~ Ellen, mom of an infant/toddler

The brand's response to these category "developments" is important. Toys "R" Us earned goodwill from Ellen with their exchange policy in the face of the baby bottle crisis. Additionally, several organizations, including EvenFlo and automobile insurers, also earn goodwill by offering programs to make sure that child safety seats are properly installed.

The impact of this constantly changing safety information is that mom is exposed to perceptually greater "risks" than her child may actually face. It can be difficult for a mom to sort through the information and understand the true risk. There is also the ability for mom to go online, view blogs, or read Twitter to check into any and every possible risk.

The resulting heightened health and safety concerns and potential hyper-vigilance are typically more pronounced among newer or first-time moms who are in "learning mode" and are receptive to any sort of information that can help them. In this environment, consumer brand names can provide the reassurance that the mom is doing everything she can for her child's safety.

> My first [child], in particular, it was really about adaptation and really doubting whether I could do it or do it right, and so I relied a lot on books and pediatricians as more of my influencer. I was just thinking back on some of the brands that I used, and it seems that I kind of went to the ones that I knew I could count on as being safe because I didn't trust my own choices, if you can imagine. But things like Pampers. . . . You know, if I was going to buy a car seat it was going to be Graco. I knew that I could trust that.
>
> ~ *Sarah, mom of a young adult (reflecting on infant/toddler years)*

Brands are very important to mom in helping her to make good health and safety choices. Another example of moms relying on the bigger brands in the health and safety area comes from Marissa's comments on her brand choices:

> We try to do all the safety precautions like baby gates and clasps on the cabinet doors. He is very curious and very mischievous. When it comes to safety stuff, I look into what is most expensive, and figure it's better.
>
> ~ *Marissa, mom of an infant/toddler*

Preschoolers

As her child moves into the preschool years, mom's focus in the area of health is around establishing healthy habits. These healthy habits include washing hands after going to the bathroom and before eating, brushing teeth, and using a tissue or a shirtsleeve when sneezing.

> She knows she has to wash her hands all the time, especially after going to the washroom, and brush her teeth in the morning and at night. The school also reinforces this.
>
> ~ *Bonita, mom of a preschooler*

Our research found that mom continues to reinforce healthy habits as her child grows older, stemming from this preschool foundation. Healthy habits for older children and young adults include getting regular check-ups and

Mrs. Meyer's Clean Day

The Mrs. Meyer's Clean Day brand offers a range of cleaning products touted as "aromatherapeutic household cleaners." In addition to offering the benefit of mood-enhancing aroma, the Mrs. Meyer's brand also offers peace of mind for some moms who want more natural cleaning options. Zola, a mom of an infant/toddler, mentioned that she is concerned with the cleaning chemicals that she uses around the house, and she has switched to Mrs. Meyer's.

> They have really good scents and clean well (except the detergent). I love Mrs. Meyer's because it's natural, and you don't have to worry about it so much. Before that, I was using vinegar to clean, but it doesn't cut grease. I'm using a lot of Mrs. Meyer's now that I have a baby.
>
> ~ Zola, mom of an infant/toddler

In addition to its general line of household cleaners and laundry room products, the Mrs. Meyer's brand also offers Baby Blossom Laundry Detergent which is "extra gentle" and "dermatologist tested to be safe for baby."[8]

Overall, the brand promises to provide "earth friendly" and "cruelty free" products that "smell like a garden," not like harsh chemicals.[9] The implication is that these products are safer for children and pets.

The Mrs. Meyer's brand has received primarily favorable reviews from online mom bloggers and the media. The main negative comments come from those who find the scent too powerful. In 2008, the Mrs. Meyer's brand was acquired by SC Johnson, demonstrating that the brand had established a unique market position with moms.

As further demonstration of success, the Wall Street Journal online calls the Mrs. Meyers Clean Day line "a surprise retail hit" and highlights that it carries a 30 percent price premium.[10]

dental visits, as well as having health insurance. The overall goal for mom is to have her child lead a healthful lifestyle and avoid preventable illness.

Similarly, mom's physical safety concerns evolve from the baby-proofing focus of the infant/toddler years to safety when outside riding a tricycle or bicycle, scooter or skateboard, or even just crossing the street. Preschoolers are cautioned to stop when they get to a street or alley and to wait for their mom or caregiver to check to make sure if the intersection is safe to cross. Bonita's comments are typical of preschool moms:

> I think that sometimes she can be a bit of a risk-taker, and we have to slow her down and explain to her, you can't do this and you can get hurt. For instance, when she comes to an alley, she needs to stop on her tricycle. One day, she didn't stop and she saw a car coming towards her. Seeing the car made a big impression.

> ~ *Bonita, mom of a preschooler*

The directions that moms provide for their preschoolers with regard to the children's outdoor safety is consistent with the guidelines suggested by the Center for Disease Control and Prevention's parental guidelines for preschoolers. These include: "Tell your child why it is important to stay out of traffic. Tell him not to play in the street or run after stray balls. Be cautious when letting your child ride her tricycle. Keep her on the sidewalk and away from the street. When your child is playing outside, keep watch over him at all times. Practice water safety. Teach your child to swim."[11]

When the preschool child gets older, mom continues to focus on bike and street safety. Brands and organizations that help with reinforcing these safety messages are much appreciated, as Yolanda's story illustrates:

> I want Manuel to be aware at this age (seven). He's been very good. I don't have to remind him at this point, he knows to look both ways and watch for cars, though I still won't let him cross the street without me. The American Red Cross comes to school once in a while, and they set up a little traffic area and have them ride their bikes within the traffic rules and look both ways before crossing the street.

> ~ *Yolanda, mom of an elementary schoolchild*

The safe "riding" progression continues with middle school moms reminding their children to wear helmets and kneepads when using a scooter or skateboard, and moms of teenagers and young adults cautioning their older children on safe driving habits.

Brands that reinforce healthy habits and safe behaviors tap into a priority focus area for these moms. For example, a toothbrush or toothpaste product that encourages the preschool child to brush his or her teeth correctly and safely will meet with mom's approval. One mom mentioned that she will buy her preschooler a toothbrush depicting a character that her child prefers to encourage her child to brush and to reinforce the healthy habit.

Elementary Schoolchildren

As the child grows beyond the preschool stage, new health and safety challenges appear even in situations where the mom has found a solution for the child at an early age. In addition, the child may begin to push back or protest against the safety measures in a way that he or she did not at an earlier age, making mom's job harder. For example, one mom we spoke to (Lila) found the more active outdoors lifestyle of her kindergarten son posed new challenges.

Lila had been aware since birth that her son had sensitive skin and had problems with products with fragrances, so she was very careful with the products used on his skin. In addition to having sensitive skin, her son's skin was fair and reacted quickly to any sun exposure. Her solution was to rely on powerful, brand-name sunscreens with SPF 45 or higher to prevent him and his older sister from getting a burn. During the early childhood years, this approach worked well for Lila, her children were compliant, and their skin did not suffer any flare-ups. The situation changed in summer 2008 when her eight-year-old daughter began spending more time outdoors at a soccer camp. Around this same time, Lila saw an online message about potentially dangerous chemicals in sunscreens that can be absorbed into the skin and are carcinogenic to mammals. She followed the Web site link to the Environmental Working Group (EWG) (www.ewg.org) and saw their summary declaring that of 952 name-brand sunscreens tested, "3 out of 5 sunscreen products offer inadequate protection from the sun, or contain ingredients with significant safety concerns." The study stated that leading sunscreen brand names, including the one Lila used, were the "worst offenders."[12]

Based on the EWG information, Lila ordered one of the highly rated, off-brand sunscreen products that used inorganic/physical blocker ingredients such as titanium dioxide and zinc oxide as their primary ingredients and avoided the more powerful active ingredients. When Lila was applying the product to her children's skin (which cost twice as much as regular sunscreen), her daughter complained that she did not like the fragrance, the white color left on her skin, or the "greasy feel," effectively pushing back against her mother. Nonetheless, Lila persisted in using the physical blocker product for both of her children. Unfortunately, her son burned very quickly using this product, and so Lila returned to using the brand-name sunscreen. In Lila's opinion, the trade-off was between efficacy in preventing sunburn and sun damage and a potential long-term health risk. When her children were younger and their activities did not require them to be outside as much, a less effective physical blocker sunscreen that was "safe" may have been a solution. However, in the elementary school years, Lila's children needed a product that could hold up to running and sweating in the sun and also wasn't unpleasant to apply.

> I tried a "safe" brand. I ordered it from the Web site and I tried it . . . and it was an SPF 30+ and that was the highest they offered. Cathleen, my daughter, is older, and she was complaining that the sunscreen smelled disgusting and left her skin with a white look. After the first day, Cathleen and Ned were burned . . . so I ended going back to the major brand. I did go to Whole Foods, and they offered California Baby and others. It was $15 for a four-ounce portion that we have gone through in about two days, and it had the same ingredients as the brand that didn't work, so it may not have worked. . . . In the end, I said, is it really worth it? Am I that concerned?

> *~ Lila, mom of elementary schoolchildren*

Safely driving her own children (and other children) in the car also continues to be a top focus area for moms in the elementary years. In fact, motor vehicle traffic accidents are the leading cause of death in children during the elementary school years and remain the top risk through middle school and high school. According to the National Center for Health Statistics, motor vehicle accidents account for 20 percent of deaths among five to nine year olds, 20 percent of deaths among ten to fourteen year olds and 35 percent among fifteen to nineteen year olds. This contrasts considerably with children under one, who are at greater risk of dying from congenital anomalies, SIDS, and respiratory diseases.[13]

While safety in the car is important to moms of elementary schoolchildren, there is conflicting information on when to use booster seats, as Lila's story reveals:

> The government standards for the booster seat . . . state that you have to use it [until] eighty pounds, pretty much regardless of height. So we

went to Cathleen's nine-year check-up and the pediatrician said, "Oh, she doesn't need a booster anymore. She should be fine, she's at the right height." So we were in an interesting situation where some of the parents at school were going by weight and some by height. Some kids who were taller than Cathleen still had to sit in the booster, and it was a complete embarrassment for them.

~ *Lila, mom of elementary schoolchildren*

The doctor mentioned that since Cathleen's height was sufficient that the chest seat belt would hit her at the shoulder, not the neck, this was acceptable. In the end, Lila made the decision to let Cathleen graduate based on the pediatrician's advice. Lila mentions that Cathleen was thrilled to be out of the car seat and viewed it as a rite of passage, bragging about it to all of her friends.

Lila reports that the pediatrician typically spends ten minutes in her child's annual checkup visits reviewing the top safety and health issues for the child's specific age. She recalls that the pediatrician specifically covers the child's sleep habits, eating habits, exercise habits, and how much television they are watching. While her pediatrician made a point to hone in specifically on not eating while watching television due to a "direct link to obesity," this wasn't new information for Lila. Instead, she was the most interested in exploring a question about food allergies. She found the food allergy question could not be addressed by the pediatrician. Lila followed up with online research and consulted other moms who have children with food allergies to find a specialist to do testing. She says that she now recognizes that the pediatrician is a generalist and has limited expertise in dietary and digestive areas. This supports the finding that other moms and Web sites are critical information sources when it comes to more specific health issues. Lila continues to consult with her pediatrician when she has questions, but she supplements his information with other sources. This suggests that online research and trusted information from friends and family members are also very important to mom when her questions become too specific for the pediatrician to answer.

The risk of being kidnapped and abused by a stranger, sometimes called "stranger danger," also receives considerable attention from moms of elementary schoolchildren, schools, and other organizations concerned with safety. Yolanda's comments illustrate this point:

I want him to be aware and to pay attention. When we are in a public place and he doesn't want me to go with him to the bathroom anymore, I want him to be aware of what's okay, nobody's supposed to touch you. Back to his karate classes, they've done a lot of training in stranger danger and also self-defense. Also, don't answer the door or the phone if you don't know who it is.

~ Yolanda, mom of an elementary schoolchild

In addition to concerns about motor vehicle safety, allergies, and weight control, pediatricians may warn mom of accidents from trampolines, roller skates, and other "lifestyle-related" injuries to which elementary schoolchildren are susceptible. What is interesting is that most moms with whom we spoke didn't have these issues top-of-mind (outside of bicycle and scooter or skateboard safety). Despite mom's lack of focus, the facts illustrate, when it comes to injuries, kids between the ages of five and nine are at greatest risk of a fall, followed by being struck by another person. These two factors account for 59 percent of all non-fatal injuries in this age category. These same two factors are also the leading causes of injury in "tweens" ages ten to fourteen, accounting for 51 percent of all non-fatal injuries. In addition, overexertion (perhaps due to sports) becomes a larger issue for kids ages ten to fourteen, contributing to 12 percent of all non-fatal injuries.[14] There is an opportunity for brands to help inform moms about the most frequent statistically-based risks and how to avoid them, and also to communicate to her greatest "perceived" health and safety risks.

Middle Schoolers

When it comes to middle schoolers, moms can be faced with more challenges in addressing health and safety concerns, as their children are older and even less compliant than they were in their younger years.

In the middle school years, it is appropriate for the child to take more risks and go outside with less supervision. Because of the constant publicity around kidnapping, mom may be fearful to allow her child to go outside unsupervised. Yet unsupervised play under safe conditions is generally suitable for middle schoolers. Amy's comments underscore these concerns:

I'm really concerned about safety, because she's at that age where she's asking now to go to the mall with her friends by herself. I'm just really concerned about trying to find a balance between letting her grow up, but also I don't want her to be fearful, but I want her to be conscientious about her surroundings.

~ *Amy, mom of a middle schooler*

In addition to physical safety, health concerns around weight emerge at higher levels in "tween" and teen years, for almost one-fifth of all children. Despite all the information on healthy diets, the fact is that an increasingly large number of American kids are now overweight. The Centers for Disease Control and Prevention (CDC) statistics report that obese children are represented in 17.6 percent of children ages twelve to nineteen in 2003-2006, 17.0 percent of children ages six to eleven, and 12.4 percent of children ages two to five. These numbers are more than double the levels found in the 1976-1980 data.[15] While few moms see being obese or overweight as desirable for their children, the culprits are well known—a combination of a sub-optimal diet and more sedentary lifestyles, encouraged by computers, television, and video games. Additionally, while weight is a concern, mom can also see her child as "safe" while indoors using the computer. There is an opportunity for brands to encourage middle schoolchildren to be active in a relevant way and to support mom in her quest for them to do so.

One approach marketers have taken is to sponsor safety and health-related programs that reach kids. For example, local State Farm Insurance agents sponsor children's bicycle safety clinics. Bicycle-related injuries are the fifth leading cause of non-fatal injuries for kids ages five to fourteen,[16] so bicycle safety programs offer a service to address this need. Many local police and fire departments also offer similar programs.

Another important area of focus related to health and safety is communication about the choices for children with specific food allergies like nuts or gluten. Frequently, every mom is made aware if a child in the class faces these challenges. Tammy's story (she is both a mom and a teacher) illustrates this trend:

> Within the last year, there has been an increased focus on instilling healthy eating habits. A group of moms worked on this, and it led to an all-new policy at school on healthy eating habits, a healthy lunch menu, and guidelines about the food that kids can eat at school. Recently, there has also been more information also on presence of nut allergies. The teachers all have to carry an EpiPen in the classroom in

case of a severe allergy reaction. Gluten is also on the rise and attention to dietary issues in general.

~ Tammy, teacher and mom

Cyber safety is an increasingly important focus area for moms of middle schoolers. The percent of these moms who find cyber safety "very important" has increased from 74 percent of moms in 2007 to 80 percent of moms in 2009.[17] Additionally, cyber safety concerns are more pronounced for moms of middle schoolers and teenagers as compared to moms of younger children.[18]

There is an opportunity for marketers to support existing programs and to develop new approaches and messaging to encourage middle schoolchildren to be safe and healthy. There is also an opportunity to support mom in encouraging cyber safety with her middle school and teenage children. Mom will appreciate brands that take the effort to help her communicate with her child in an age-relevant, contemporary way.

Teenagers

When it comes to teenagers, moms' concerns for safety include heightened focus on the dangers of alcohol and drugs, as well as their potentially deadly combination with unskilled teenage drivers. Yet for many moms, the convenience of having their child be able to do some of his or her own driving compensates for safety concerns. Carlotta's story illustrates this dilemma:

> Matthew's (age eighteen) main problem right now is driving; he's had two fender benders in six months. At least he hasn't hit anything living yet. Having him drive is convenient for me, and it's convenient for him. For instance, he just got done with basketball practice, so other kids would have to bring him home if he didn't have a vehicle. He also uses his car for his pizza delivery job. My role as a mom has really changed now that he's a teenager and driving. When [my children] were little, we were going to sit down and do crafts and play together, and when they became teenagers they were going to love each other and we'd do stuff together; that was the vision. The reality is now, the main part of my duty is just cooking them supper and doing the laundry.

~ Carlotta, mom of teenagers

Technology has combined with inexperienced drivers to pose new threats. Alicia's comments on texting illustrate this point:

> One of the things is driving with the cell phone and the texting on it and paying attention while driving. I point it out and send it if there is something on the news. I sent all three of my children an e-mail today about a crash that a young girl was texting while driving. That is a big safety thing.

~ Alicia, mom of teenagers

In addition to concerns about teenage driving, mom's concerns about drug and alcohol abuse accelerate during the teenage years. We see this in the *State of the American Mom (SOAM)* study, where moms rate their concerns about drug and alcohol use by their child(ren) as a highly important area of concern and focus, just behind physical safety and ahead of cyber safety.[19] There are a variety of religious, community, and health organizations that encourage parents to talk with their children about the consequences of drug and alcohol abuse. Disturbingly, however, in some qualitative interviews we led with middle schoolers and young teenagers, they told us the most engaging brand commercials are for beer.[20]

The facts are that more than one-third of deaths in the teen years (ages fifteen to nineteen) are caused by motor vehicle accidents.[21] This presents an opportunity for brands to connect with both mom and the teen if they can successfully help the teen be a better driver or avoid dangerous situations (e.g., do not ride with a friend who is drinking, have a designated driver, etc.). Despite all this messaging, teens tend to consistently overrate their own driving abilities, giving themselves nine out of ten on their driving skills in all road conditions, despite having been driving only a few months.[22] Some brands, like State Farm and Allstate, have gone out of their way to develop programs encouraging responsible driving to teens. The State Farm Steer Clear program offers mom age-relevant message points as well as a team safety program, as the case study illustrates.

Another concern area for teen moms that we spoke to includes safe sex. One mom mentioned that her goal for her teen and young adult daughters (she has three) is to finish school without getting pregnant and having a baby. She says, "I talk to them about not having children. The goal is to for my daughter to finish her schooling. The guy she is with would like her to have kids, but I want her to wait." Another mom of a teen boy men-

State Farm Insurance

State Farm Insurance, the largest automobile insurer in the United States, is committed to promoting teen auto safety. State Farm's approach is to partner with parents, teens, and their own agents to promote safer teen driving. State Farm makes its message authentic for moms and teens with initiatives that offer a local connection through State Farm agents in addition to broader, national efforts. The company's "Steer Clear" program encourages safer teen and young adult driving because traffic crashes are the biggest cause of death for teens in America.[23] Qualifying teens must practice driving under parental supervision, take a self-assessment, and watch an instructional video to enroll in the program, which provides a 15 percent discount on their automobile insurance policy.[24]

As part of the Steer Clear efforts, State Farm used social media to connect with moms and become a partner in informing teens about safe driving habits. For example, on its Facebook page, State Farm previously included a hub for moms to discuss teen driving and to share tips about effectively speaking with their children about safe driving. State Farm and The Children's Hospital of Philadelphia researched optimal strategies for parents in speaking with their children to create these tips.[25] The Facebook initiative reinforced State Farm's brand image as a "caring neighbor" by helping to enable family conversation about safe driving. With these initiatives, the company forges an emotional bond with mothers that goes beyond the discount. According to State Farm spokesperson Vicki Harper, parents find the biggest benefit from enrolling in the program is to make sure their children are safer on the road.

This approach has worked for the company. Harper said enrollment in the Steer Clear program is growing, and State Farm has introduced new features to make enrollment easier for moms and their children. In February 2010, State Farm introduced a free mobile application that would track the teen's driving time and provide them with safety tips.

"Parents have told us that they need more information about guiding their teen through the learning to drive process," said State Farm Vice President for Strategic Resources Laurette Stiles in a news release.[26]

State Farm (continued)

"This new application provides trip suggestions, goals and pointers for assessing driving skills. By providing this tool, State Farm hopes to support supervised practice and improve teens' skills for independent driving."

State Farm and its agents organize local initiatives to encourage safer teen driving. For example, in the Mid-Atlantic region, agents created interest in the program by offering a dollar bill and marketing materials to all high school students who drove into a high school parking lot with their seat belts buckled.[27] These local initiatives tie into a national Teen Driver Safety Week campaign (held annually in October) to raise awareness for safer teen driving through local awareness movements and media publicity. Through their safety involvement, State Farm agents show a local, tangible commitment to social responsibility. As a result, State Farm is able to elevate its image through credible means.

State Farm reinforced its brand's caring image through authentic, grassroots, and national efforts to reach both teens and their moms to promote auto safety. By creating an emotional bond with moms, State Farm has increased enrollment in its Steer Clear program and has boosted its image among moms as a company that helps her take care of her children.

tioned that although she doesn't believe he is sexually active, she goes out of her way to be sure that she has talked to him about safe sex as a precaution. Since this is a tough area for mom to discuss with her child, she will appreciate brands that promote safety in this area in a way that will grab the attention of her teen.

Young Adults

As children move from the teenage to young adult years, the paradigm shifts because these children are now moving out on their own to college and beyond. There is a pull and push as to how involved the mom can be when it comes to her children. She still wants to keep them safe from the world, but she also needs to give them independence to figure things out. Mom is ingrained with the instinct to always protect, so at this stage she is very often forced to go against her natural tendency and allow her child to make decisions that may be harmful. Many adult children no longer live under the mom's roof, so there is much less direct control for mom to keep her child safe. This provides an increased challenge and opportunity for marketers as moms of young adults do still have influence, but they are trying to figure out how to define the relationship.

> The main thing I am concerned about as they are adults is drinking and driving. They've never had any trouble, but I'm very cognizant of the fact that they like to drink. When my daughter turned twenty-one, I sat her down and said, you need to not drink and drive and to have a designated driver. I've discussed that there is alcoholism on both sides of the family. Every weekend when she goes out, she's heading to a party. Recently, she told me that they are going to a party and have booked a hotel room there as she is probably going to get trashed.

> ~ *Diane, mom of young adults*

There are real threats to her child's safety for moms of young adult children. The biggest mortal risks for young adults is motor vehicle accidents. Among young adults ages twenty to twenty-four, 26.9 percent of all deaths in 2006 were caused by motor vehicle accidents. A similar motor vehicle accident death rate is seen among teenagers ages fifteen to nineteen at 25.2 percent, whereas children ages ten to fourteen only had a 4.3 percent mortality rate. Other issues are homicide at 16.5 percent of deaths among young adults ages twenty to twenty-four, and suicide at 12.1 percent.[28] In addition, moms of young adults also cite that many of their biggest concerns relate to sex, including unwanted pregnancy and alcohol and drug use/abuse. For moms of young women, there is also a heightened awareness around rape and date rape drugs.

This group of children has a very unique health concern relative to other age groups—lack of health insurance. Also of concern to moms is that these young adult children may not place a high priority on obtaining health insurance, even when they become parents themselves. They have been dubbed "young invincibles" by insurance companies—people who do not opt for health insurance either because they feel "bulletproof" or they cannot afford the cost. Margarita's comments about her adult daughter, age nineteen, who now has a child of her own, illustrates this point:

My goal is that she has health insurance for herself and her son. My daughter says we really don't need it, we don't go to the hospital that much. I say do you know the emergency room itself is a $100 co-pay. I look at her, with her child, and she doesn't understand it's important.

~ Margarita, mom of a young adult

Nearly one-third of nineteen to twenty-nine year olds are currently uninsured—they are the largest uninsured segment of the population. Young people are likely to lose health coverage at two junctures—when they graduate college and when they are discontinued from their parents' policy (on average around age twenty-three). Due to unemployment and lack of jobs that offer healthcare, the number of uninsured college graduates is more than 2.5 million.[29]

This issue may become somewhat less problematic for parents and young adults, because parents may now be able to continue to provide some health protection for their children—under the new health care legislation, young adults are able to stay on their parents' insurance until age twenty-six. The Tonik example points out the results that a brand that addresses this gap can garner.

The young adult years are a challenging time for moms who will always be concerned about their children's health and safety, but who also need to disengage from direct involvement. Brands that help mom provide her young adult child with useful advice and suggestions in the area of health and safety will be rewarded given the close relationship many Millennial young adults have with mom.

Conclusion

Safety and health concerns are hot-button issues for many moms as one of mom's most important roles is to protect her child's life and health. This protectiveness is a central, defining role for moms. Safety and health concerns remain prominent in moms of all ages, but the level of concern decreases as the children move from infant stage (highest concern) to early childhood and then elementary school and middle school. In the high school years, moms may not voice as many immediate health and safety concerns, but new concerns arise and/or take on more prominence, such as drug and alcohol abuse, safe sex, and teenage driving, which becomes a major "hot-button." Unfortunately for mom, the health and safety concerns for her teen child

Tonik

Anthem Blue Cross Blue Shield (owned by WellPoint) recognized the opportunity to serve the young adult market and launched Tonik, a health insurance plan aimed at the uninsured youth with three levels (thrill-seeker, part time daredevil, and calculated risk-taker).

Tonik uses edgy and modern marketing to reach its target consumers. For example, its Web site is a flash page with a bold-colored background and shadow outlines of young twenty-somethings, an image that recalls the popular iPod commercials. The consumer is shown pictures of active young adults listening to music or snowboarding. These images help connect Tonik with the idea of freedom, because the young adult consumers are freed from traditional high-cost insurance.

In addition to reaching out to young adults, Tonik recognizes the influence parents most likely have on persuading children to opt for health insurance as well as evaluating plans. As a result, Tonik's blog provided information that highlighted why its plans are a good option for young adults, even in light of the new healthcare legislation.[30]

This business strategy has proven to be successful for WellPoint. Tonik is currently offered in California, New Hampshire, Colorado, Nevada, and Georgia Over three-quarters of Tonik's enrollees in those states were previously uninsured according to company data .[31]

However, the plan is not without its critics. John Garamendi, then-lieutenant governor of California, criticized the Tonik plan for failing to adequately serve its target population, specifically for failing to cover pregnancy.[32]

But WellPoint claims that Tonik provides a valuable service to Americans who might not otherwise have been able to obtain the service: "The programs are working—approximately 75 percent of Tonik members were previously uninsured. Through all of our individual plans, over the past two years WellPoint has provided coverage to 750,000 Americans who were previously uninsured."[33]

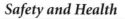

THEME RESOURCE GUIDE

Safety and Health

	Mom's Concern For Her Child	Mom's Concern For Herself
Infant/Toddler Moms	• Physical safety • Adult supervision	• No strong concerns
Preschool Moms	• Physical safety • Adult supervision	• No strong concerns
Elementary School Moms	• Playground/ sports safety • Stranger danger	• No strong concerns
Middle School Moms	• Cyber safety • Sports safety	• No strong concerns
Moms of Teens	• Teen driving, drinking, drugs, sex ed	• Disease prevention/ control
Moms of Young Adults	• Some concerns around driving • Health insur- ance coverage	• Disease prevention/ control

■ = Higher Mom's priority
▨ = Moderate Mom's priority
☐ = Lower Mom's priority

don't diminish, but her control over them does. Young adults' safety in the world is still of utmost importance to the mom.

The Theme Resource Guide: Safety and Health provides a reference for a brand to use in exploring this important theme area for moms.

Some brands, like State Farm Insurance with its Steer Clear program, are offering "honest talk" for moms in addressing her needs for health and safety for older children. Other brands, like Mrs. Meyer's, help mom by providing her with the peace of mind of natural cleaning options, which seem safer for young children and pets. Additionally, the Tonik Insurance brand has directly addressed the need for greater health insurance coverage among young adults. Significant additional opportunity remains for brands to connect with moms and, as appropriate, with their kids around safety and health issues.

Notes

1. Marketing to Moms Coalition, *State of the American Mom* 2009.
2. Ibid., mom interviews.
3. Marketing to Moms Coalition, *State of the American Mom* 2010.
4. Ibid.
5. EvenFlo, "Safety Made Easier," accessed May 15, 2011, http://www.even-flo.com/sme_full.aspx?id=294.
6. Juvenile Products Manufacturers Association, "JPMA Certification Process," accessed May 15, 2011, http://www.jpma.org/content/safety/certification-process.
7. Rachel L. Gibson, *Toxic Baby Bottles: Scientific Study Finds Leaching Chemicals in Clear Plastic Baby Bottles*, Los Angeles, CA: Environmental California Research and Policy Center, 2007.
8. "Baby Blossom Laundry Detergent—64 Loads," accessed May 15, 2011, http://www.mrsmeyers.com/products/laundry/baby_blossom_laundry_detergent_-_64_loads.
9. "Our Story," accessed May 15, 2011, http://www.mrsmeyers.com/our_story.
10. Anne Marie Chaker, "The Pampered Countertop," February 9, 2011, accessed May 15, 2011, http://online.wsj.com/article/SB10001424052748704364004576132081767603482.html.
11. "Child Development: Preschoolers (3-5 years old)," accessed May 15, 2011, http://www.cdc.gov/ncbddd/child/preschoolers.htm.

12. Environmental Working Group, "Finding the Best Sunscreens," accessed January 16, 2010, http://www.ewg.org/whichsunscreensarebest/2009report.

13. United States, Center for Disease Control, Division of Vital Statistics National Center for Health Statistics, "Infant, Neonatal, and Postneonatal Deaths, Percent of Total Deaths, and Mortality Rates for the 15 Leading Causes of Infant Death by Race and Sex: United States, 1999-2006," pp. 1-23.

14. Centers for Disease Control and Prevention, "Injuries Among Children and Adolescents," accessed January 11, 2010, http://www.cdc.gov/Ncipc/factsheets/children.htm.

15. Centers for Disease Control and Prevention, "U.S. Obesity Trends by State: Trends by State 1985-2009 (Related Resources)," accessed May 15, 2011, http://www.cdc.gov/obesity/data/trends.html#Related.

16. Centers for Disease Control and Prevention, "Injuries Among Children and Adolescents," accessed January 11, 2010, http://www.cdc.gov/Ncipc/factsheets/children.htm.

17. Marketing to Moms Coalition, *State of the American Mom* 2007, 2009.

18. Ibid., 2009.

19. Ibid., 2007.

20. Insight to Action, confidential interviews 2009.

21. Centers for Disease Control and Prevention, "Teen Drivers: Fact Sheet," December 3, 2009, accessed January 11, 2010, http://www.cdc.gov/motorvehiclesafety/teen_drivers/teendrivers_factsheet.html.

22. Insight to Action, confidential interviews 2005.

23. State Farm, "Teen Drivers. Honest Talk. Real Solutions: A Handbook for Parents," accessed May 15, 2011, http://www.betterteendriving.com/young_driver_handbook.pdf.

24. Jeffrey, Wilson, "Steer Clear Program: State Farm Young Driver Discount," December 21, 2007, accessed May 15, 2011, http://meridianstar.com/columns/x681097281/Steer-Clear-program-State-Farm-young-driver-discount.

25. Personal interview with Vicki Harper, June 15, 2010.

26. "Teaching Your Teen to Drive? New State Farm Mobile Application Can Help," February 25, 2010, accessed June 15, 2010, http://insurancenewsnet.com/article.aspx?id=166678&type=propertycasualty.

27. Personal interview with Vicki Harper, June 15, 2010.

28. National Adolescent Health Information Center, "2006 Fact Sheet on Mortality: Adolescents & Young Adults," accessed May 15, 2011, http://www.pacwcbt.pitt.edu/curriculum/202AdolIssRskRsl/Appndcs/App1_Mrtlty.pdf.

29. Kevin Quinn, Cathy Schoen, and Louisa Buatti, "On Their Own: Young Adults Living Without Health Insurance," The Commonwealth Fund, May 2009, http://www.commonwealthfund.org/~/media/Files/Publications/Fund%20Report/2000/ May/On%20their%20Own%20%20Young%20Adults%20Living%20Without%20Health%20Insurance/quinn_ya_391%20pdf.pdf.

30. Naya Jones, "Tonik Health Insurance: Still a good option for young people?" March 24, 2010, accessed May 15, 2011, http://www.medicoverage.com/tonik-blog/tonik-health-insurance.

31. "Tonik Fast Facts," accessed May 15, 2011, http://www.anthem.com/wps/portal/ahpculdesac?content_path=shared/noapplication/f0/s0/t0/pw_ad088005.htm&label=Tonik%20Fast%20Facts&na=pressroom&rootLevel=4.

32. "California Insurance Commissioner Challenges CDHC, Rebuttal Data Offered," accessed May 15, 2011, http://www.hsafinder.com/California-Insurance-Commissioner.

33. "WellPoint, Inc. 2006 Summary Annual Report," accessed May 15, 2011, http://media.corporate-ir.net/media_files/irol/13/130104/reports/wlp_2006_AR_v2.pdf.

CHAPTER 6

Technology: Texting, Talking, Teaching

Our research indicates the relationship with her child and the quality of the communications with her child are mom's top two priorities.[1] We find that technology enables mom in two ways. The first is to help her communicate with her child, caregivers, and significant others. Today's technology allows for communication in more ways than have ever been possible (e.g., through Skype, texting, and Facebook). Many moms feel that technology has allowed their family life to be as close or closer than their families were when they grew up. In fact, a recent Pew Research Center study indicates that 25 percent of adults feel that their family is closer because of the use of the Internet and cell phones.[2] The second way is to help her accomplish tasks more effectively and even make her life easier. The map feature on the iPhone is a good example of this convenience, so mom doesn't have to locate directions before leaving her house.

Many moms also believe that it is important for them to stay on top of the latest technologies, both to communicate with their children in the way that is most savvy, and as a tool to juggle their busy lives. In our interviews, we found most moms are highly "wired," using cell phones with texting and e-mail features to communicate real-time information, both with their kids and with other caregiving adults (e.g., dads, coaches, and teachers). These technologies help moms navigate complicated family calendars with working parents, divorced parents, blended families, and myriad extracurricular activities. Marissa's comments illustrate this point:

> I use a lot of technology; I use the Blackberry, cell phone, laptops . . . to keep it all together. I send Outlook appointments to my ex-husband, and he accepts them for their [kids'] calendars. . . . I think e-mail has

been very helpful for us, too. It's a very non-emotional way for [us] to connect about things for the kids. I cannot believe I am the kind of mom who actually has cell phones for both girls, but it's just worked for us. My oldest prefers the texting option. She's just in that mode and she's at that age now where she'd prefer not to be on the phone talking to her Mom—it's kind of not cool.

~ Marissa, mom of a middle schooler and high schooler

Among moms with whom we spoke, the cell phone was the most popular technology for helping to manage their personal lives and stay in touch. Several reported recently getting a phone with a QWERTY keyboard to make texting much easier. Other popular technologies are Facebook, Web sites like Freecycle.org and Craigslist.com, Skype/video chatting on the computer, Wii, the iPod and the iPhone, and computers and the Internet in general. In our interviews, none of the moms reported spending a lot of time reading or publishing blogs. This is consistent with quantitative research that shows publishing, reading, and participating in blogs touches only 15 percent of moms.[3]

While some of the technology tools are shared between moms and their child(ren), such as text messaging, a 2009 Pew Research Center study found that teenagers are cutting back on blogging as a mechanism and rarely using Twitter, leaving blogging and Twitter as the provenance of adults. Specifically, only 14 percent of teens ages twelve to seventeen were blogging, and only 8 percent use Twitter, while 73 percent use social networks, particularly Facebook.[4] Instead, the moms with whom we spoke reported using cell phones, texting, instant messaging (IM), Facebook, and Skype with their teen and adult children.

Many moms also enjoy keeping up with other moms, friends, and family online, with many claiming to very often or sometimes share jokes (44 percent), upcoming events (49 percent), inspirational phrases (42 percent), video/images (41 percent), and news clips (41 percent).[5] Marissa's comments speak to this sharing approach among moms:

With my friend Karly, she has a little boy just two weeks older than my daughter, so we talk all the time, and IM stuff. We've been best friends now, and it was really nice going through the pregnancy and bouncing off ideas. We usually IM or text back and forth.

~ Marissa, mom of an infant/toddler

Infants/Toddlers

Moms of infants/toddlers are very actively involved with technology. It is hard to say which is more important to them: their cell phone, which is a lifeline to caregivers, husbands, and others in their "village," or their computer, with its myriad useful and entertaining applications. As the iPhone case study on the next page illustrates, moms of infants/toddlers find the iPhone particularly appealing as a "one-stop shop" for texting, calling, e-mails, Internet, Facebook, and applications (apps) with which their young child can play.

As figure 6.1 illustrates, moms of infants and toddlers are using their computers for many practical reasons, including e-mailing, checking weather, reading news, researching, shopping, entertainment, and many others.

Moms of infants and toddlers, especially first-time moms, are the group most likely to use blogging as a way to communicate their experiences and to connect with the outside world at a time when their life is focused intensely on their young child. In fact, 20 percent of moms of infants/toddlers are reading or publishing blogs. This compares with 20 percent of moms of children ages three to six, but only 12 percent of moms of teens ages thirteen to seventeen. Moms of infants and toddlers are the most likely age segment to use Facebook (69 percent of moms of infants/toddlers used Facebook in 2010, compared with 59 percent overall).[6]

At a 2008 "mommy blogging" conference in New York, a panel of leading mom bloggers talked about how blogging and tweeting fit into their lifestyle and provide an outlet for their creativity. Some of these moms also hope that these activities will result in future career options and compensation. Several mom bloggers also mentioned that they no longer read a newspaper, and instead gets their news through social media.

Given the size and buying power of the mom market, many brands are actively working with mom bloggers. The goal is to connect with these influential moms in order to better market new products and services, and to get the group's feedback on existing products and services. Bloggers at the Mommy Dialogues Conference were clear that for a brand to be successful in building a relationship with them, it requires a commitment to an ongoing human resource (person) to focus on the relationship. The blogger moms preferred that the representative be inside the organization versus an outside organization, like a public relations agency. One example given by these moms was the former Zappos.com CEO, Tony Hsieh, who utilized

iPhone

Technology companies like Apple can win mom's loyalty by creating intuitive interfaces that mom can use to entertain her child and to help her in a multitude of ways. Apple, known for its innovative technology interfaces, is so ultra-friendly that it markets toddler apps for its iPhone product on its Web site. In our interviews, moms reported that their eighteen-month-olds can use these applications and operate the iPhone. Reviews on Apple's Web site and our own research confirm that toddlers are able to use these apps easily because of the intuitive touch interface.

Several moms with whom we spoke agreed that the toddler iPhone applications were very easy to use. They mentioned that their children can use the iPhone before a computer as it does not require a keyboard.

Zola, the mother of twenty-one-month-old Ebben, said her daughter was able to start using the iPhone when she was fifteen months old.

> Ebben uses the coloring book app on the iPhone. She knows where the stickers are, and she can color with one finger. As soon as we got the iPhones, the kid's applications were among the first we got. Another thing we use the iPhone for is to jump on YouTube to show her some videos.

> *~ Zola, mom of a toddler*

Another mom, Julie, said her two-year-old son Andrew is able to fully manipulate the iPhone. "One day, we just handed it to him as we were busy and wanted to keep him busy," Julie said. "He started using this at eighteen months old."

In addition to keeping kids busy and entertained, mom finds the iPhone's features appealing because it helps her juggle all of her responsibilities. The easy access and intuitive nature of these features is key for mom because the iPhone can help her cut out time-consuming steps in her busy schedule.

Moms with whom we spoke indicated the iPhone is very helpful with its QWERTY keyboard for texting, and the iPhone can replace a camera and camcorder for photographing their child.

iPhone (continued)

"Every parent could use a hand," the Apple Web site says. "Keep up with your kids or just keep them busy with family-friendly iPhone apps."[7]

One mom of a toddler (Zola), who has a low household income, explained that the iPhone is a priority. To save money, she shops at thrift stores and buys discount groceries. She does not pay for Internet access or any cable or satellite television options. Yet the iPhone is indispensable. Zola likes the iPhone because of the many features that help simplify her life. Whenever she is worried about her toddler daughter's health, Zola surfs the Internet on her iPhone to find the information she needs. Zola said she also uses her iPhone as a camera and a camcorder as a way to keep connected with friends and family. "We can record our daughter's life on the phone and send it from there," Zola said. "We send it to family and friends who live out of state."

Meanwhile, Julie said she appreciates the ease of receiving and sending text messages on the iPhone due to its QWERTY keyboard. Since Julie works, her sister takes care of Julie's son, Andrew. Julie and her sister text each other to keep informed of anything they need to know to care for Andrew. Julie appreciates receiving text updates from her sister before she arrives to pick him up so she can efficiently manage her daily schedule. "It's great because before, when he was at day care, when you picked up your child, you got a report, and there was never time to read it," she said. "It's always hectic when you're picking up the kids. I prefer getting text messages during the day."

Apple has leveraged its interface to reach busy moms who want to keep their children entertained while they juggle their daily responsibilities. Moreover, by offering time-saving iPhone features, Apple is able to elevate its image among these busy moms.

FIGURE 6.1. ACTIVITIES YOU CURRENTLY DO ON THE INTERNET BY AGE OF OLDEST CHILD (2010).

Activity	Total Moms	Moms with Oldest Child Age 2 and Under	Moms with Oldest Child 3-6	Moms with Oldest Child 7-12	Moms with Oldest Child 13-17
Checking/sending personal email(s)	65%	64%	64%	62%	67%
Paying bills/other online banking	54%	50%	62%	53%	51%
Checking weather	48%	45%	49%	47%	50%
Reading news	48%	47%	48%	48%	47%
Using social networking websites (e.g., Facebook, Twitter, Linked In)	47%	56%	50%	43%	46%
Downloading coupons	39%	40%	41%	40%	38%
Researching products/brands (including price comparisons)	37%	39%	39%	35%	36%
Shopping for myself	35%	40%	38%	32%	33%
Playing games online	34%	28%	37%	34%	34%
Researching health/medical topics	34%	43%	35%	32%	32%
Shopping for my child(ren)	34%	38%	41%	34%	30%
Buying gifts for others	29%	32%	29%	32%	26%
Planning travel	29%	29%	25%	33%	28%
Checking/sending work-related email(s)	26%	26%	25%	23%	30%
Purchasing/listening to music	25%	28%	24%	25%	25%
Viewing/posting photographs	25%	36%	30%	25%	21%
Researching diet/nutrition	24%	26%	23%	24%	24%
Working	24%	29%	21%	22%	25%
Help kid(s) with their homework	23%	2%	9%	31%	29%
Watching videos	23%	27%	23%	21%	24%
Networking	18%	24%	21%	17%	15%
Shopping for my spouse	18%	25%	22%	21%	14%
Publishing/reading/participating in blogs, bulletin boards, message boards	15%	20%	20%	13%	12%
Sending electronic invitations	9%	15%	10%	9%	8%

Twittering and was accessible to his customers for regular problems and issues. The mom bloggers found this highly appealing.

Mom bloggers, brands that manage Twitter feedback, and other online marketing experts also stress that if a brand or organization chooses to establish a channel for consumer feedback and opinion, the organization must be prepared that not all the feedback will be positive, and be prepared to work this through, often under extreme time pressure. While there are clear challenges and risks, the frequent use of the Internet as a leading information resource for moms highlights the necessity for infant and toddler mom-focused brands to allow moms to engage with them using today's technology.

Thus, Apple's iPhone has a double appeal: fun and useful for mom and entertaining for her child. In fact, the iPhone is so helpful and valued that for some moms it is a priority ahead of more expensive clothing, food, or Internet access in their home. At the same time the iPhone is so user-friendly that a toddler can use the device. A mom of an infant/toddler, with her intense desire to share and connect around this lifestyle, uses myriad technologies in addition to the iPhone and will continue to be a heavy use and adopter as new technology options emerge.

Preschoolers

Like other moms, the moms of preschoolers with whom we spoke are using the top two technology tools of the Internet-enabled computer as well as the cell phone to communicate, be entertained, do research, shop, and connect. Moms of preschoolers with whom we spoke also reported that they value using e-mails to receive information from their child's day care or school and to communicate with the teacher, as Bonita's remarks demonstrate:

> Usually the school sends me e-mails with special events and announcements. I do e-mail the school. When I write the school, I'll e-mail the teacher with a question, and she's pretty good about responding. This works well for me as a mom. On the other hand, I am a teacher, and when I need to get in touch with the parents, I will usually call and get them to come in as I typically need to speak with them urgently.

> ~ *Bonita, mom of a preschooler*

In addition to e-mails, moms of preschoolers also use texting to communicate. Texting is particularly valuable to the many moms who do not have Internet access or data plans on their phones. For those moms, sending an e-mail while on the go isn't practical, and a phone call can be difficult in working settings, as Bonita's and Yolanda's statements describe:

> I am doing more of it—the texting. When we're out and about, and we don't have the Internet on our phones, it's much easier. I've been with a new phone with the QWERTY keyboard for four months now. I was starting to text more with my husband, sisters, and friends and found I needed a new phone, and thought why not get one with a keyboard?
>
> ~ *Bonita, mom of a preschooler*

> I am huge text messager. Honestly, when I am at work in the hospital, I can't whip out the phone and talk on it. I got a QWERTY keyboard to make it easier to text. I am mostly texting my mom because she watches my son most of the time. It took about a month to get my mom into texting, but now she texts more than I do. In several ways texting is better. If you can't access the e-mail for some reason, mom can always get a text message. It's more reliable. A typical text message might be "Make sure he gets his medicine" or "I'll be late."
>
> ~ *Yolanda, mom of a preschooler*

Comparing the Internet activities of moms of preschoolers with moms of infants shows that the former are slightly less likely to view or post photographs (36 percent of moms of infants/toddlers compared with 30 percent of moms of preschoolers). Instead, moms of preschoolers are more likely to play games online (37 percent of moms of preschoolers versus 28 percent of moms of infants/toddlers).[8] Some of these behavioral changes may reflect the fact that moms are taking somewhat fewer photos of their children as they get older. These behavioral changes are also likely driven by the return to work of many moms of preschoolers. As we can see, texting solves a problem for many preschool moms who need to stay in contact with their child's caregiver, but who may not be allowed to talk or feel comfortable talking on the phone in the workplace.

Elementary Schoolchildren

Technology is omnipresent in the everyday lives of elementary schoolchildren and their moms. And, unlike their preschool counterparts, many elementary schoolchildren have the reading skills and manual dexterity to engage using "adult" technologies like computers. Mickey's story illustrates how her elementary school sons are following in her footsteps using the iPod.

The most helpful technology for me is music and the iPod because I am a fitness instructor. I have my own iPod and a speaker to go with it. iTunes and iPod are the best because my older boys (ages eight and eleven) have inherited one of my older generation iPods. We don't really let them use the iTunes account, but we will put songs they want on it from all the CDs my husband and I have.

~ Mickey, mom of elementary schoolchildren

Moms of elementary schoolchildren can have mixed emotions around their child's technology use. On the one hand, moms are often encouraged by pediatricians to limit screen time, whether in front of a television, computer, cell phone, or video game. Often, these moms are also concerned with limiting the child's access to inappropriate content. On the other hand, moms recognize that the "play" for their child on the computer or video games can be educational as well as an entertaining, with numerous choices including mathematics, foreign languages, reading/writing skills, fantasy worlds, music, art, and more. With the advent of technology like Wii Fit, Guitar Hero, and Dance Dance Revolution, video games are also working to combat mom's negative perception of screen time's sedentary nature.

Lila's story illustrates the mixed thoughts that many elementary moms face around technology:

We limit screen time. Right now we don't have a dedicated computer for the kids. I am consciously holding off mostly because my son (age seven) is insatiable with electronics. By not having a computer, it's just been easier for me to restrict it. But my thoughts are changing. Over this Thanksgiving holiday, we were at my sister's who has three computers for the kids. She has a lot of kid's programs like math or Freddie Fish. I was looking at that thinking well, okay. Not having to deal with constant pressuring from my son, we would give him an educational game, the kids would go off, and I had a lot of talk time with my sister and husband. Come to find out the kids are playing these games together, and they're really happy. We have talked about it and maybe we'll get a computer. And the school has recommended programs, like Zoombinis as educational.

~ Lila, mom of elementary schoolchildren

In addition to computer games, online games, and iPod use, elementary schoolchildren also play video games on dedicated gaming systems like Xbox 360, PlayStation 3, and the Wii. In addition, there are handheld systems like Nintendo DS. In the *State of the American Mom* (*SOAM*) research, video games were one of the top areas that kids are allowed to choose themselves, particularly among multicultural moms.[9]

Among moms of elementary schoolchildren, almost one-third report they are going online to help their child with his or her homework. Their children are also gaining familiarity with the computer at school and may use it to watch and play games, as Yolanda's comments illustrate:

> The computer is almost mandatory in every school. He is so proficient on the computer. He will do the Yahoo video chat with his father right now. I can set it up and leave him to do it himself. He will also go to the Web sites for the show he watches on Nickelodeon, and they have games. Another thing is the Wii. This has helped him with his manual dexterity by using the control.

> *~ Yolanda, mom of an elementary schoolchild*

Among moms of elementary schoolchildren with whom we spoke, there was mixed acceptance of the need for a cell phone for their child, unless the child had a challenging and varied schedule or a shared custody situation. Many moms of elementary schoolchildren do not have a problem with the concept of their child eventually getting a cell phone; they just do not recognize a significant need in the elementary school years. As recently as 2007, approximately 50 percent of moms would not consider a cell phone until their child was at least thirteen, although 23 percent did consider it for ages ten to twelve.[10] Most recently, however, Pew Research found a trend to mom acceptance of children owning cell phones at younger ages, with 58 percent of twelve year olds reporting owning cell phones in 2009.[11]

Moms of elementary schoolchildren are also using Facebook to stay in touch with and share pictures and advice with family and friends who live further away. Corkey's comments illustrate this:

> I use Facebook to talk to my family in Salina [Kansas] and Nebraska. For instance, with one of my cousins, the topic of being a mom has come up. She is kind of new at being a mom, so I have given her advice on what needs to be done.

> *~ Corkey, mom of an elementary schoolchild*

Moms also reported using Facebook to plan family events and to stay in touch with their own mom (the grandmother).

While there is a real question on whether her elementary schoolchild should have a cell phone, there is no doubt for mom's personal need. Moms of elementary schoolchildren find the cell phone essential to stay in contact with their caregivers. Corkey's comments are typical:

> My cell phone is my way of keeping in contact with anybody I need to when I'm not at home. I use Facebook at night to play on the computer, but the cell phone is more important because that's the way I communicate if I call or text. I do more of my communication on the phone than the computer. I can't use a computer at work. So, during the day the cell phone is all I have. I use the computer just at night.

~ Corkey, mom of an elementary schoolchild

When asked to identify brands that are doing a good job informing moms about relevant technology products and services, moms of elementary schoolchildren specifically mentioned cell phone plans for families. They also mentioned that *Scholastic* magazine (distributed in schools) highlights specific software as educational, such as Zoombinis. Teachers are also a trusted information source for these moms on appropriate computer programs. The Educational Products Inc. (EPI) case study demonstrates one brand's success in marketing through the school channel and providing additional convenience, through technology, to moms of elementary schoolchildren. EPI built a business around making it easier for moms to tackle back-to-school shopping. Elementary moms also tend to rely on recommendations with other moms (including online recommendations) to gather information on specific technology products and services. Marketers trying to reach this group are well served to employ word-of-mouth marketing approaches, in addition to traditional methods.

Middle Schoolers

While technology is accepted as a natural part of everyday life for most moms, it also comes with heightened concerns for the cyber safety of middle school and teenage children in particular. As children in the middle school years turn more to peers as an important influence source, and then interact with these peers using text, IM, and other technologies, moms of middle schoolers realizes that their control is diminished. Even though some schools offer courses on cyber safety, mom realizes that this training may not always be taken to heart and that her child may be overconfident in his or her ability to evade cyber stalking and bullying. As a priority for moms, the topic

Educational Products Inc.

Late every summer, before the first autumn leaf falls, moms face the task of outfitting their elementary schoolchildren for the return to the classroom. In many cases, elementary schools and teachers have prepared detailed supply lists for parents. Specialty retailers like Office Depot and Office Max set up distinctive sections to expedite back-to-school shopping. It is important to recognize, however, that school supplies represent only a portion of mom's back-to-school spending as there are other major back-to-school categories like clothing, shoes, sporting equipment, textbooks, and computers. In fact, clothing accounts for the largest portion of mom's back-to-school spending (30 percent), while school supplies represent just 14 percent.[12] To the extent that schools have chosen to dictate the lists, school supplies and books offer little or no choice or discretion on mom's part, rather, gathering the items is a chore.

Several online organizations have developed to make the school supplies shopping process more convenient for moms, and to potentially offer better pricing through quantity discounts. In many cases, these organizations even deliver the supplies directly to the school, making the whole process even more convenient for mom and eliminating shipping charges.

Moms can order supplies and books online from predetermined lists and select from choices that the school and/or teachers have selected. For example, Educational Products Inc. (EPI) is a company dedicated to helping moms and schools streamline the supply gathering process. Founded in 1979 by a school principal, it now considers itself the "nation's number one custom school supply program, [offering] a variety of fundraising programs, custom apparel and science fair projects."[13] Kory Davis, director of sales and marketing at EPI, explains that "these programs are most popular among elementary school moms and offer the convenience of getting school supply shopping done in five minutes."[14] In a typical school, 35 percent of moms will participate the first year that EPI offers its services, and frequently this number rises to 90 percent of moms after four years, once moms have gained familiarity with the service. Moms order supplies online and through tradi-

CASE STUDY

EPI (continued)

tional paper-based forms, depending on the school.[15] Organizations like EPI offer benefits of convenience for mom. These organizations have used technology to make moms' lives easier by cutting out supply gathering chores. Even during the recent recession, EPI reported continued growth. The firm is expanding by now offering additional services to moms who are doing school fund-raising.

of cyber safety becomes more important in middle school and teen years.[16]

While cyber threats from strangers receive media attention, moms also notice risks from other children, especially "friends." For example, one mom of a middle schooler that we interviewed had a daughter who was being cyberbullied by her "girlfriends" from school. Extremely hurtful comments about her daughter were instant messaged by one of the girls in her daughter's clique. Then the other girls in the group joined in. In addition, inappropriate content was forwarded via e-mail by one of the girls to the others. When we asked the mom why she did not restrict or terminate her daughter's access to these damaging messages, her response was that she did not want her daughter to be cut off from the social circle. This example illustrates that these communication technologies create new concerns among moms for the emotional well-being of their middle school kids as well as opening new doors for communication between parent and child.

By the time their children reach the middle school years, many moms have also opted to provide them with a cell phone in order to make it easier to keep in touch. Alicia reflects on how she has given her middle school daughter, Alex, a phone at a much younger age than her oldest child, and an even younger age for her youngest child. Alicia also mentioned getting the Nintendo Wii.

> I didn't use a cell phone with my oldest since he is from another generation (thirteen years older). But this generation, my youngest got a cell phone by age eleven. Her sister Alex got it at age fifteen. Alex didn't ask for it, but she did traveling with the Color Guard, and so I wanted her to have it. Now she is into texting, and I was paying so much because she exceeded the limit. So, we got the unlimited family plan. We

did get the Wii for the family pretty much. We do the bowling, and the golf [on the Wii] as a family together. Both of my daughters asked for [the Wii] for Christmas.

~ Alicia, mom of a teenager and a middle schooler

The Beatles: Rock Band provides a good example of how a gaming technology can bring together moms and their children. While this game has broad appeal across age of kids, its greatest impact is likely among moms of middle school and older elementary school children.

Teenagers

As children become teenagers, they reach out even more to their peers, and the multitude of new communication technologies facilitate more dialogue in more ways than was ever possible before. According to a recent Pew Research Center study, 85 percent of teens ages twelve to seventeen engage at least occasionally in some form of electronic personal communication, which includes text messaging, sending e-mail or instant messages, or posting comments on social networking sites.[17] Another Pew study found that cell phone texting is preferred by teens as the number one communication channel. The same study found 54 percent of teens who own cell phones sent text messages daily, while only 11 percent e-mailed on a daily basis.[18] And mom is using these technologies to communicate with her teen.

We find that moms of teens are highly attuned to these technological changes, at times because their teen has encouraged them to try new approaches. Specifically, several moms shared that their teen helped them set up a Facebook account and also encouraged them to text message. Several moms mentioned that their child would far rather that she text message them instead of calling on the cell phone. This is because the text message is more "hidden," whereas the teenage child's friends could observe a voice-to-voice phone interaction.

Moms tell us that text message and cell phone marketers stand out as doing a good job of portraying teen and mom communication in a humorous and appealing way. From a product perspective, the ubiquitous "family plans" allow moms to add their child(ren) to their basic service plan for reduced costs, and this enables the communication. Moms with whom we spoke struggled to find examples outside of phone and text service providers that offer products that help families and also portray parent/teen relations

The Beatles: Rock Band

CASE STUDY

The Beatles: Rock Band succeeded because it created a family experience by bringing parents and children together through the music of the Beatles.

The Beatles: Rock Band was released on September 9, 2009. The game allows up to four players to play guitar, bass, drums, and to sing vocals for the forty-five Beatles songs included in the game. According to the *New York Times*, the game was important because it allowed the entire family to interact while enjoying the timeless music of the Beatles.[19] Moreover, the game was a major turning point for Beatles fans because it was the first time the Beatles agreed to let their tunes be sold in a digital format.[20]

To market the game, MTV Games partnered with Paul McCartney, Ringo Starr, and the widows of George Harrison and John Lennon to create and design the characters' looks throughout the band's career. Moreover, McCartney and Starr helped launch the game the day before the Electronic Entertainment Expo (E3) video game conference in Los Angeles in June 2009 by holding a surprise appearance to inform the public about the game's release. McCartney commented that he loved the game.[21] Their endorsement helped generate buzz and excited the audience about the game's release.

Harmonix Music Systems, the Cambridge, Massachusetts-based game developer of Rock Band, said the games were equally accessible to parents and children. Harmonix Creative Director Josh Randall told MediaPost, "We discovered it wasn't just teens—but also parents and younger children. And we wanted The Beatles: Rock Band to invite people into the game that [they] had never played before."[22]

This strategy of helping families become part of the Beatles experience created a positive buzz due to the interactive experience.

This ability to bring people together was critical to the game's success, according to MTV Games. In May 2010, it was reported that the Rock Band video game has reached nearly 2 million video game units sold, according to MTV Networks.[23] The estimated $20 million Rock Band marketing and advertising campaign is considered highly successful.[24]

Rock Band (continued)

The Beatles: Rock Band was able to use technology to bring parents and children together. The communal game-play and the popular music helped MTV Games generate sales and reach a wider consumer base than if the company had merely targeted teens or high-involvement gamers.

and communications in an appealing way. Instead, there are many brands that choose to appeal to teen independence and rebellion.

> The advertising for the cell phones and all that—they're pretty funny! You see that and you think, oh yeah, that could be my situation. They will show the parents figuring out how to text, and they'll be at the table where the parents will be texting, and the kids are like "okay, that's enough of that." It's tongue in cheek and speaks to both the teenager and the mom. You don't see many commercials like that. In fact I can't think of any others.

> ~ Amy, mom of a teenager

Isabel's story illustrates how her older teenage son encouraged her to use Facebook and MySpace:

> The first time Justin went to Iraq, he called me up and said, "I need you to get started on MySpace," so I could upload photos of the kids for him. Now, this is another way to communicate with my kids, using Facebook and MySpace.

> ~ Isabel, mom of a young adults

2010 Marketing to Moms Coalition research showed that more than 50 percent of moms of teenagers use Facebook, while less than 20 percent of moms of teenagers use MySpace,[25] and the numbers are increasing rapidly for Facebook.

In the social teenage world, cell phone pictures are often uploaded to Facebook accounts and tagged within a few hours after the event or even during the event. For example, pictures from a high school party may be posted online within hours of the party's end, so that the experience can be shared and revisited. While taking pictures at a party is nothing new, the immediacy of easily sharing these images with a broader social network is relatively unprecedented. And often, mom is doing the same.

> The only thing my kids are really big on is their cell phones. They do texting, Facebook, and upload pictures. And my kids showed me [this]. So I said, okay, I need a phone [like that].

~ Isabel, mom of young adults

In addition to online and cell phone technology, teenagers are highly involved in the world of gaming. According to the Pew Research Center, video gaming is pervasive—97 percent of teens play games. This holds true among young and older teens, girls and boys, and teens from across the socioeconomic spectrum. For most teens, gaming is a social activity, which they play with others. Three-quarters of teens play games with others at least some of the time. Teens also play frequently, with 50 percent indicating they played the day prior to the survey. Additionally, they use multiple platforms to play games: computers (73 percent), dedicated consoles like Xbox, PlayStation, and cell phones/PDAs (48 percent).[26] Parents claim to engage in some sort of monitoring of this gaming, with 90 percent of parents saying they always or sometimes know what games their children play, and 72 percent saying they check the ratings.[27] With the video game rating system of "M" level games, mom can feel a little safer knowing that she will need to be present in the store for her child to buy these games.

Mom and her teen are highly engaged with technology and use it to maintain frequent communication with each other.

Young Adults

As children move into young adulthood, technology represents the same dichotomy for parents and children—an easier way to keep in touch, even at times too easy. Years ago, when children went off to college, it was a big step in terms of independence. In the past, moms may have expected to talk with their children once or twice a week. In recent years, however, moms are increasingly staying in much more frequent contact with their young adult children. In fact, 50 percent of young adults in a recent Pew Research Center study, ages eighteen to twenty-five, report being in touch with their parents on a daily basis, with contact via phone as the most popular method.[28]

In terms of which parent is communicating with these young adults, mom is the primary anchor for the family. Among adults with both parents living, 61 percent say they have the most contact with mom, only 18 percent with dad, and 21 percent report the same contact with both parents. [29]

Margarita's comments about staying in touch with her young adult daughter illustrate this frequent contact:

> Lately we've been doing texting. My daughter is a little worrywart. If I'm not at home, she wants to know where I am. I tell her where I am at or I tell her I'm going somewhere and when I'll be back. We don't have a set routine so we keep in touch with texting.

> *~ Margarita, mom of a young adult*

Isabel reports that her children will ask for her help when they and she are both at work.

> I know all the software programs. I use Word. They call and ask me how to do things.

> *~ Isabel, mom of young adults*

Today's young adults are unique from older adult groups in that they grew up with technology. It has always been part of their lives. Additionally, these young adults keep in contact with their moms more than previous generations. Technology has enabled these close relationships and more frequent communication. Moms of young adults use these technologies to stay in touch and provide ongoing support to their children. For instance, a mom of a young adult that we interviewed e-mailed favorite family recipes to her twenty-year-old daughter who was living overseas, and she then coached her daughter on how to make the recipes step-by-step using Skype. There is an opportunity for organizations to reinforce mom in "cyber" support of her children, and also to humorously depict, as appropriate, mom learning these new approaches from her young adult children or even turning the tables by teaching them a trick or two.

Conclusion

In our conversation with moms, technology was a huge "hot button." Moms cite the help that technology provides with keeping up with their busy lifestyle as a major benefit. Based on their comments, it seems that both the QWERTY keyboard cell phone and the Internet-enabled computer are mom's best friends. Importantly, mom recognizes that these tools allow her to communicate with her child in new ways that were not possible in the

Skype

CASE STUDY

Skype is a popular telephone and videophone software service (www.skype.com) that allows people, including moms and their adult children, to inexpensively stay in touch. All Skype computer-to-computer calls between subscribers are free, and there are also options that are telephone-based. Use of Skype has climbed steadily since its introduction in mid-2004, and as of mid-2011, Skype reportedly had 170 million connected users. In May 2011, Microsoft agreed to buy Skype for $8.5 billion. [30]

There are many stories of moms using Skype to stay in touch with remote family members and share the latest developments in their lives. An example comes from Susan, who uses Skype to call her in-laws each week. Susan and her husband, Rob, set up Rob's parents in Italy with a webcam and Skype so that "Nonno" and "Nonna" can share in their granddaughter's lives.

> Every Saturday morning, we call Italy computer-to-computer through Skype. Julia loves to show off her toys to her little cousin Emily and say "ciao" to all her aunts and uncles. It means so much to us that Julia can still be seeing her family in Italy every week and really knowing who they are. She constantly talks about Nonno and Nonna, and her memories of being there on their farm stay fresher when she can see and talk to them regularly.

> ~ *Susan, mom of elementary schoolchild*[31]

When an adult child is highly mobile (e.g., when touring a foreign country), Skype can play a useful role. We met a mom of a twenty-one-year-old who proudly reported that her daughter used Skype and McDonald's free Wi-Fi service in Europe with her netbook to keep her mom posted of her travels. Skype appears to be leveraging this consumer insight, as their 2008 advertising campaign featured a young adult traveler who regularly posted her exploits each day. Specifically, the campaign focused on twenty-six-year-old Rebecca Campbell and her round-the-world adventure travel.[32]

Another example comes from our interview with Julie, a mom of an infant/toddler. Julie reported using Skype to keep in touch with her

CASE STUDY

Skype (continued)

husband on a daily basis while he served in Iraq.

> My son has grown up with technology. When he was a baby
> and my husband was deployed, we would get on Skype every
> day. So as a baby, he saw his dad every day on Skype. When my
> husband came home from deployment, Andrew recognized him
> because he saw his dad on Skype. It was the greatest thing ever.

~ Julie, mom of a toddler

Skype's marketing approach during its early years has been well documented. The first focus was on a benefit known to have great appeal to moms—namely, a product that works well and is easy to use. As Nils Hammar, a former Skype employee, writes in his 2007 research paper "Skype: Reasons for Growth," documenting the early history of Skype, "The first version of Skype's website was just as simple as the software. No technical or complicated words—focus on getting people to understand the benefits, and download and try out the product. The original tagline was simple: 'Free Internet Telephony that Just Works' . . . the focus for the development team was all about 'delighting the user,' and to making sure usability and call quality kept improving."[33]

As noted in ithink:

> Skype understood the relevance and importance of its website and
> made it simple, usable and focused to provide its audience with
> the information they needed. They added a forum to involve people to discuss ideas and views on how the product can be evolved.
> Once the product had been well recognized, they started using
> their website to sell other value-added services.[34]

Skype drove its growth with a combination of public relations and viral marketing. The Skype case example presents a number of helpful marketing tactics in involving users in marketing and in focusing their technology products on ease of use in order to achieve success with both moms and young adults.

THEME RESOURCE GUIDE

Technology

	Mom's Concern For Her Child	Mom's Concern For Herself
Infant/Toddler Moms	• Entertainment (e.g., iPhone)	• Communicate with adults • Share entertain, research
Preschool Moms	• Entertainment • Education	• Communicate with adults • Share, entertain, research
Elementary School Moms	• Entertainment • Education	• Scheduling, mapping, organizing
Middle School Moms	• Entertainment • Check in with mom	• Lifeline to child starts
Moms of Teens	• Check in with mom • Entertainment	• Lifeline to child continues
Moms of Young Adults	• Lifeline between parent and child	• Lifeline to child continues

■ = Higher Mom's priority
▨ = Moderate Mom's priority
▢ = Lower Mom's priority

past. Karen's comment illustrates how technology helps mom remain connected with her child:

> Technology is all across the board. Whether it's cell, text, or a larger, faster computer and a bigger screen . . . technology [like texting], allows you to be connected when you aren't close by or you don't want to be a hovering "helicopter mom."

~ Karen, mom of middle schooler and teenager

Since the relationship with her child is mom's number one priority, followed by communication with her child, the technology products and services that help mom achieve this goal will be rewarded.

The Theme Resource Guide: Technology will give the reader a quick summary and reference tool to consider when a brand is exploring the technology area. For example, we can see from the Mom's Concerns for Herself column of the guide that starting at the middle school years, the cell phone becomes mom's lifeline to her child. By comparison, mom's technology concerns for herself in the preschool years center on communicating with other adults as well as sharing, with friends, entertainment and research online.

Several brands have addressed mom's reality in their marketing, including cell phone family plan providers, iPhone, The Beatles: Rock Band, and Skype. While mom may sometimes think that her older children learn new technologies faster than she does, she quickly adapts to new equipment. With the close relationship of the young adult to their parents, we see technology truly going in both directions, child to mom and mom to child. This presents an opportunity for brands to humorously recognize and celebrate parent and child technology collaboration.

Notes

1. Marketing to Moms Coalition, *State of the American Mom* 2009.
2. Tracy L. M. Kennedy, Aaron Smith, Amy Tracy Wells, and Barry Wellman, *Networked Families: Parents and Spouses are Using the Internet and Cell Phones to Create a "New Connectedness" that Builds on Remote Connections and Shared Internet Experiences*, Washington, DC: Pew Internet and American Life Project, 2008, pp. ii-iii.
3. Marketing to Moms Coalition, *State of the American Mom* 2010.

4. Amanda Lenhart, Kristen Purcell, Aaron Smith, and Kathryn Zickuhr, "Social Media & Mobile Internet Use Among Teens and Young Adults," Pew Internet and American Life Project, February 3, 2010, accessed 5/19/11, http://www.pewinternet.org/~/media//Files/Reports/2010/PIP_ Social_Media_and_Young_Adults_Report_Final_with_toplines.pdf.

5. Marketing to Moms Coalition, *State of the American Mom* 2010.

6. Marketing to Moms Coalition, *State of the American Mom* 2010.

7. Apple, "Apps for Moms and Dads," accessed June 17, 2010, http://www. apple.com/iphone/apps-for-everything/momsdads.html.

8. Marketing to Moms Coalition, *State of the American Mom* 2010.

9. Ibid., 2009.

10. Ibid., 2007.

11. Amanda Lenhart, Kristen Purcell, Aaron Smith, and Kathryn Zickuhr, "Social Media & Mobile Internet Use Among Teens and Young Adults," Pew Internet and American Life Project, February 3, 2010, accessed 5/19/11, http://www.pewinternet.org/~/media//Files/Reports/2010/PIP_ Social_Media_and_Young_Adults_Report_Final_with_toplines.pdf.

12. Marketing to Moms Coalition, "Back to School Highlights" 2010.

13. Educational Products Inc., accessed May 20, 2011, http://www.educationalproducts.com/aboutushome.htm.

14. Personal interview with Director of Sales and Marketing for Educational Products Inc. Kory Davis, February 11, 2010.

15. Ibid.

16. Marketing to Moms Coalition, *State of the American Mom* 2009.

17. Amanda Lenhart, Aaron Smith, Alexander Macgill, and Sousan Arafeh, (2008). *Writing, Technology and Teens,* Washington, DC: Pew Internet and American Life Project, 2008, p. ii.

18. Amanda Lenhart, *Teens, Cell Phones and Texting*. Washington, DC: Pew Interest and American Life Project, 2010.

19. Seth Schiesel, "All Together Now: Play the Game, Mom." *New York Times*, September 6, 2009, p. AR1.

20. Tom Lowry, "Video Games: Will the Beatles Rock MTV?" August 6, 2009, *Business Week*.

21. Daniel Radosh, "While My Guitar Gently Beeps," August 16, 2009, *New York Times*, p. MM26.

22. Anne Mai Bertelsen, "Come Together, Right Now, Over Rockband," September 8, 2009, http://www.mediapost.com/publications/?fa=Articles. showArticle&art_aid=113089.

23. Beth Snyder Bulik, "Entertainment A-List No. 5: The Beatles, Rock Band: Simultaneous Launch of Re-Mastered Catalog and Game Creates Powerful Sales Combo," *Advertising Age,* May 24, 2010, accessed May 20, 2011, http://adage.com/print?article_id=143999.

24. Ibid.

25. Marketing to Moms Coalition, *State of the American Mom* 2010.

26. Amanda Lenhart, Joseph Kahne, Ellen Middaugh, Alexander Macgill, Chris Evans, and Jessica Vitak, *Teens, Video Games and Civics*, Washington, DC: Pew Internet and American Life Project, 2008, p. i.

27. Ibid.

28. Andrew Kohut, Kim Parker, Scott Keeter, Carroll Doherty, and Michael Dimock, "How Young People View Their Lives, Futures and Politics: A Portrait of 'Generation Next,'" Pew Research Center, January 9, 2007, accessed May 20, 2011, http://people-press.org/http://people-press.org/files/legacy-pdf/300.pdf.

29. Paul Taylor, Cary Funk, Peyton Craighill, and Courtney Kennedy, "Families Drawn Toge4ther by Communication Revolution," Pew Research Center, February 21, 2006, accessed May 19, 2011, http://pewsocialtrends.org/files/2010/10/FamilyBonds.pdf.

30. "Microsoft to Acquire Skype," May 10, 2011, accessed May 19, 2011, http://www.microsoft.com/presspass/press/2011/may11/05-10corpnewspr.mspx.

31. Susan Carraretto, "Merry Christmas from 5 Minutes for Mom and Skype," accessed May 19, 2011, http://www.5minutesformom.com/5223/skype/.

32. Mark Selfe, "Around the World with Skype Marketing Campaign," May 8, 2008, accessed May 20, 2011, http://www.redherring.com/blogs/24226.

33. Nils Hammer, "Skype—reasons for growth," master's thesis, Stockholm School of Economics, February 2, 2008.

34. ithink "Skype–Marketing Brilliance and Use of Website," November 21, 2005, accessed May 19, 2011, http://www.ithink.in/skype-marketing-brilliance-and-use-of-website/.

CHAPTER 7

Fashion and Beauty: Sweater-vests Be Gone!

From the time a new baby enters a woman's world, she is advised to take care of herself: nap when the baby naps; eat well and stay hydrated, especially when nursing; let your friends baby you the first week or so of your child's life; do not be afraid to ask for help.

For most women, though, the reality is that parenting doesn't leave a lot of time or money for pampering. Or does it?

As children grow beyond the intensive-need years and grow into the more independent "tween" years, many moms reawaken to themselves and are more likely to indulge. These moms take a greater interest in their appearance as well as their social and emotional well-being.

"It's important [the kids] know I also have a life, and in some way they have to fit into my life as much as I've needed to fit into theirs," said Melissa, a forty-year-old insurance company executive and the divorced mother of girls ages eight and twelve. As consumers, however, many moms continue to make spending choices that put themselves last.

State of the American Mom (SOAM) research shows that when it comes to shopping habits, moms are more likely to choose value over quality in several areas, including 45 percent of moms who will sacrifice quality on clothing for themselves. In contrast, when it comes to her kids, mom is less likely to scrimp on clothing (only 27 percent will sacrifice quality to get a better value of clothing for her kids).[1] Moms across all subgroups will sacrifice the quality of her own clothes (45 percent of moms say they are willing to sacrifice quality for a better value). As we will see from the Suave case study, there is an opportunity for brands to connect with mom and help her break the paradigm of sacrifice to stay within the budget.

FIGURE 7.1. EVERYDAY ITEMS WILLING TO SACRIFICE QUALITY TO GET A BETTER VALUE (2010).

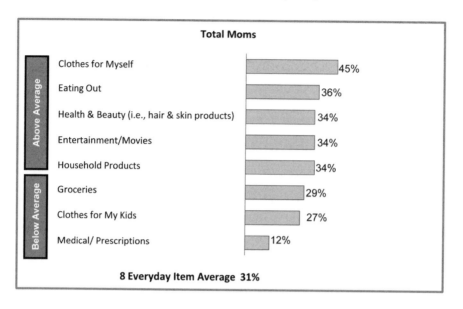

	Clothes for Myself	Clothes for My Kids
Total Moms	45%	27%
Single Moms	44%	23%
High Income Moms ($75,000+)	42%	26%
Full-Time Employed Moms	48%	29%
Oldest Child Age 2 and Under	48%	25%
Oldest Child Age 3-6	46%	28%
Oldest Child Age 7-12	42%	26%
Oldest Child Age 13-17	46%	28%

These spending habits do not necessarily correlate with socioeconomic standing. Even high-income moms are nearly as likely to make quality sacrifices on clothing for themselves; specifically, 42 percent of high-income moms (defined as more than $75,000 in household income) made this sacrifice versus 45 percent of all moms. Interestingly, this sacrifice does not correlate to working status, as 48 percent of full-time working moms also made this sacrifice. On the other extreme, single moms—maybe hoping for a return on investing in themselves—are less likely to sacrifice the quality of their own clothing for value.[2]

In addition to being highly value conscious and recognizing product benefits like quality, mom values and responds to brands that touch her emotions or, at least, acknowledge them. Moms respond best to marketing that shows a mom having fun with her kids, that makes moms laugh, that acknowledges the multitasking life of moms, or that offers suggestions on healthier ways to live.[3]

In 2007 Suave found a way to make an emotional connection with mom, as the case study illustrates.

Infants/Toddlers

As Suave uncovered in its repositioning research, mothers of newborns—and some women through the span of their child's early years—are apt to say they have lost all sense of personal style. They are so busy investing themselves in nurturing children that they feel they have lost this piece of their identity. As mom of an infant/toddler Ellie notes, "I never appreciated the old cliché of 'a baby changes everything' until I was a mom. From your body shape to your priorities to the time you wake up on the weekends, it's all new. I realized that all of the changes that happen can define you, if you let them. I like to think of these changes as a chance to reinvent myself." As we have seen, this transition plays out in consumer terms as mom makes personal sacrifices (e.g., in clothing for herself) in order to support the financial well-being of her family. This does not necessarily mean, however, that mom is completely happy with the situation.

Body image weighs heavily on the minds of many young mothers. Melissa, now forty, describes her pre-baby life as one that was self-centered, independent, and full of volleyball. When her two girls were infants, her life changed.

Suave

While beauty brands may find it hard to reach women whose priorities shift after having children, Suave was able to reposition itself from being a value brand to a quality beauty brand that moms choose by forging a highly relevant emotional connection with them.

For several years prior to its repositioning, Suave had owned a value brand position through its tagline "Can you tell?" that referred to the fact that there was no quality difference between Suave and a more expensive brand of shampoo.[4] The brand had an explicitly functional value position because it was interested in reaching budget-conscious women who wanted a quality shampoo.

In 2007 Suave created big news by establishing an emotional bond with mothers through its repositioning campaign. The campaign connected with moms on an emotional level by leveraging the insight that women tend to downgrade beauty as a priority when they become mothers, because they feel guilty if they prioritize taking care of themselves. However, Suave reported that moms said they felt happier, more attractive, and more self-confident when they cared for their own needs.[5] Hence, Suave tried to reach moms by speaking to them as women who fulfill multiple roles.

The brand told moms that using Suave doesn't require them to choose between being a mom and looking attractive. Rather than sacrifice on necessities for her kids, mom could stay within her budget with Suave and still feel pretty due to the fact that Suave was a value brand whose performance was indistinguishable from more expensive beauty products. This positioning is apparent on the brand's Web site, which states, "Suave believes you can have model hair and be a model mom. Our perfectly performing, well-priced products can help moms everywhere."[6]

According to brand strategist Marcelle Saporta, Suave had to walk a fine line in this communication strategy, because the brand could not take a negative or accusatory tone with moms. Rather, the campaign acknowledged that motherhood requires a shift in priorities, and the company helped forge emotional relevance with moms. For example,

Suave (continued)

the copy in one 2009 ad that shows a picture of a mom with a mop on her hair reads, "When listing her priorities, the average mom ranks doing the floors higher than doing her hair," and closes with the tagline, "Say yes to beautiful without paying the price."[7] Generalized references to "motherhood" and the use of endearing words like "mommy" in the campaign made the message more approachable for moms.

This 360 campaign launched an unprecedented online show called *In the Motherhood*. Suave engaged moms by asking them to submit webisodes based on their true stories, and the company successfully established two-way communication with moms. Due to heavy media promotion through print and television integration, the site was the fourth most popular Web site visited by moms when it was live.[8]

The repositioning helped elevate Suave's performance credentials among women and especially moms. Suave saw a rise in its key brand indicators, approximately a 50 percent increase in the proportion of moms claiming that Suave is "a high quality brand."[9]

I got in a funk when I didn't lose the [pregnancy] weight. I'd been incredibly athletic before that, and I started to slip into more of that "mommy mode." I dressed more like a mom and didn't take care of myself as much. I found it very difficult to be as selfish just finding the time, but that was not without resentment.

~ *Melissa, mom of middle schoolers*

Ellie found comfort in Stroller Strides, a national chain she describes as "really taking off":

Stroller Strides is a workout class (a good one too!), where you bring baby in the jogging stroller and work out with the kiddos right there with you. We sing songs like "The Wheels on the Bus" while doing crunches, lunges, arm resistance, etc. It's attracting tons of moms, both working and stay-at-home (many franchises have evening classes for working women). Class eliminates the need for day care and allows you to work out with your children present (demonstrating the value of

exercise at such a young age and giving you more time with your children). After each class, we all stick around and socialize, talking about
kids that were up all night, where the latest sales are, bed-wetting (kids,
of course). It's more than a workout to women like me; it's a strong
social outlet (founded on fitness) and therapy to chat and get fit with
women that are in the same place in life.

~ Ellie, mom of an infant/toddler

Quantitatively, moms of infants/toddlers show differences from moms of
other age groups relative to the type of marketing approaches that they find
most appealing. Specifically, they are less likely to relate to the image of a
professional/working mom than other groups, likely because fewer of them
are working. Instead, they are much more likely to prefer that marketers
show a stay-at-home mom who is "put together."[10]

Mothers of infants find themselves starved for time and, in many instances, adjusting to a new body image and to new financial realities. Retailers who can help mom find good value and support her multitasking with
one-stop shopping will win her dollars. As Marissa (the mother of a two-
year-old) notes, "Normally, I'll go to Target for something else, and then I'll
wander into clothing."

Retailers can also win mom's dollars through her child. Moms of infants/
toddlers are concerned about outfitting their children. In fact, the quantitative data shows that mom is less willing to make a quality sacrifice on her
child's clothing than on her own.[11]

> I just want him to be comfortable. I want him to look cute. I don't want
> to send him to day care in jeans and a sweater because that's not going
> to be comfortable. Most of the stuff we buy comes from Kohl's/Jump-
> ing Beans—$5 for a shirt and $5 for shorts. We also like the Children's
> Place, but it's more expensive. Their stuff lasts, and it's something dif-
> ferent. It's a little more fashionable than basic.

~ Julie, mom of an infant/toddler

As mentioned previously, Julie is driven by value and pragmatism, knowing
the child may soon outgrow the clothes.

The infant/toddler years present an opportunity for brands that help
mom achieve a "put together" look with value pricing. For her children,
mom wants quality, comfort, and ideally something to show their individ-
uality. Value remains important, but brands like Children's Place are helpful, as are Target and Kohl's.

Preschoolers

Life is busy for moms of preschoolers. Fashion and beauty is not a top priority, but mom is highly conscious of body image and may attempt to begin a more serious fitness regimen that she discarded during the infant/ toddler years. This concern about weight may lead to physical activities for both mom and child(ren), even if her household income is low. Zola, the mother of a twenty-one-month-old girl whose annual household income is less than $35,000, plans to buy a pool pass so she and her husband can swim laps and then put the baby in the kiddie pool. Other moms, like Marissa, whose son is one, turn to exercise DVDs to balance child care and self-care. "I try to exercise for at least thirty minutes a day before he gets up. This keeps me sane," Marissa said. "If I don't do it before he gets up, I'll do it while he's eating using the DVD called "Turbo Jam." It is amazing you can do this anywhere." Marissa shops for herself at Kohl's (a store that was mentioned by other women for its low prices) "because sometimes I have trouble dropping a lot of money."

Bonita, whose child is three, works full time as a teacher. She shops at Ann Taylor Loft for the clothing she wears to work, favors Gap for its comfortable and casual look, and Nordstrom for the trendy and casual clothing she wears on weekends. "I don't consider myself the most fashionable person, but when I shop at these places I feel good. It makes me feel like I'm keeping up with new looks," she said.

When it comes to clothing for her children, moms of preschoolers typically follows a similar approach to moms of infants/toddlers. Stores like Target, Kohl's, and J. C. Penney are favored. As with restaurants that cater to a young child by providing distractions through coloring books or play areas, retailers who help mom by helping to keep her child entertained while she shops may capture incremental dollars from this group.

Quantitatively, moms of preschoolers are by far the most attracted to a marketing approach that shows a "contemporary" mom. In comparison, moms of infants/toddlers are the most attracted to a marketing approach that shows a "put together" stay-at-home mom.[12]

Elementary Schoolchildren

Mom's struggle with body image and weight spans all age groups. Yolanda, the mother of a seven-year-old boy, is a former basketball player who describes herself as overweight. She encourages her son to be active and spends time swimming with him.

> I want to have the endurance and stamina to keep myself healthy long enough so years down the road it's not an issue. I'll usually go to the gym or exercise bike or now that it's gotten warmer, we go swimming.
>
> ~ *Yolanda, mom of an elementary schoolchild*

Mom may find, too, that the demands on her time increase as the children branch out into extracurricular activities. This means less time for mom. Sarah, whose only child is a twenty-one-year-old son, held her head as she recalled his childhood:

> When Ronnie was in elementary school, my slogan was "the arranger," because you're trying to arrange everything. You're arranging things for school. He got into Scouts, and you're arranging all of that stuff. He did multiple sports at all times, and you're arranging all of that stuff. You're arranging the summer camp experience because you work full time, and you can't be home in the summer. You have to put him in different camps. You're always arranging everything, lining everything up.
>
> ~ *Sarah, mom of a young adult (reflecting on the elementary school years)*

Gillian, whose four children are in elementary school and middle school, confirms that she has little time to think about her wardrobe or shop for new clothes. She has adapted by perfecting the blitz shopping method, preferring stores like J. Jill, Ann Taylor Loft, Sundance, and Hot Mama.

> Since I've become a mother, I don't have much time to think about fashion or shop. I used to love to shop around. Now, I've narrowed my clothes shopping down to a few stores. I visit those few stores infrequently and buy everything I need all at once. The salespeople probably think that I'm a great customer, but they don't realize that I probably won't be back in their store for another year. I guess you could call me a binge buyer. Needless to say, my wardrobe has taken a turn away from high fashion and toward comfortable clothes that are easy to care for.
>
> ~ *Gillian, mom of elementary schoolchildren and a middle schoolchild*

Quantitatively, moms of elementary schoolchildren represent the norm or average of total moms when it comes to how they like to see mom portrayed. As such, the most popular choice for them is of a contemporary mom.[13]

Middle Schoolers

As children grow into the teenage years, the role of mom as consumer takes on an added dimension; their children have become fully brand conscious. By the time they reach high school, both boys and girls are aware of and prefer certain brands. Middle school represents a transition time, typically with the girls maturing earlier and becoming more involved with their own image than the boys.

A walk down the halls of most high schools is an advertiser's dream with brand names on full parade: American Eagle, Abercrombie & Fitch, Ed Hardy, and Victoria's Secret Pink. For moms of middle schoolchildren, there is more consideration of their child's taste in clothing. As one mother we interviewed puts it: "It's my girls' choices now, but it's my credit card." This means that products must now appeal to two demographics. Victoria's Secret (Pink) and Target are top contenders among moms that we spoke to in this segment.

As children grow older, they wield more influence over purchases, especially in larger families. This has tangential influence on purchases mom may make for herself, with mother-child shopping trips to Target as one good example. Victoria's Secret is also cited by moms as having done a good job at welcoming them as women and also capturing the teenage girl market with its Pink campaign.

> Victoria's Secret does a great job for me as a woman. To me, it feels like they transitioned their Pink Line by having it right up front in their stores where there are lots of young girls. Their intimate apparel is in back. I don't feel bad about going in there as a mom. They made it like, "this isn't all about naughty stuff." I go there with my daughters now. I never would have before.
>
> ~ *Melissa, mom of middle schoolers*

Not only do women like Melissa value feeling and looking good, they also value feeling alive and having fun. "I am not," Melissa said emphatically, "the typical sweater-vest-kind-of-wearing mom." Instead, she aligns with Apple and Target, whose ads she describes as funky, sophisticated, and cool. "I want to be the mom who has an iPod and understands how to download songs," she said.

Target caters to the new "hip mom" demographic, not only through creative advertising, but also by creating an overall shopping experience. It has become a go-to destination for mother-daughter shopping, a popular bonding experience among women of all ages. Target's wide selection of fashion, from infant to adult, makes the brand popular with moms who have children of different ages. Mickey, whose oldest child is eleven, favors Target's Circo brand for her children.

> Target has a really good selection of more inexpensive clothes, they are well made and really cute. Their Circo brand is really good and a really good price. It is one of the places where I know I can always find something because they have a good selection. And they've done a good job of keeping things trendy or fashionable. The quality holds up well.
>
> ~ *Mickey, Mom of middle schooler, elementary schoolchild, toddler, and infant*

Moms like Melissa, who travels frequently for her job, are image conscious and want to be portrayed as such in advertisements. However, for mothers who have made the choice to stay at home, image has become equally important.

> Almost all the moms on my street are stay-at-home moms. They're always out and running and staying fit. When I hear them talk, they're very much into style and fashion. They're watching E! and Bravo and *America's Next Top Model* and *What Not to Wear*. There are so many messages for them to see during the day about being hip, not dowdy.
>
> ~ *Melissa, mom of a middle schooler*

Teenagers

Image is clearly important to moms of all ages. They watch television programs about fashion. They talk to each other about trends. And they respond to marketing that acknowledges these interests.

Image is, of course, highly personal. Not all women want to be flashy. For Carlotta, the mother of boys ages twelve, sixteen, and eighteen, and a devout Christian, her style and spending habits are largely influenced by her religious beliefs.

For Carlotta, the more conservative style of Eddie Bauer, which she describes as traditional and long-wearing, appeals to her to the point that she says much of what she wears comes from that merchandiser. Abercrombie & Fitch's approach—its catalogue adorned by a racy cover wrapped one year in cellophane—caused such distaste in this consumer that she returned Christ-

CASE STUDY

Target

Target caters to the busy mom who wants to stay trendy through its creative advertising and its overall shopping experience for both moms and kids.

Target offers fashionable choices for moms at affordable prices. For example, the retailer has built a roster of international designers like Mossimo and Liz Lange, a maternity wear designer, who have provided clothing lines to be sold exclusively at Target. This initiative has increased Target's credibility in offering fashionable clothing and accessories at reasonable prices.

"Design for less," Target's Web site states. "It's what Target delivers to its guests with on-trend fashion and accessories at affordable prices."[14]

Moreover, in 2009, Target introduced a new marketing strategy that showcased real moms talking about their experience shopping at Target.

"Our new broadcast campaign reflects real moms," said Kathryn Tesija, executive vice president for merchandising at Target. "This more direct and genuine approach to broadcast marketing shows moms telling personal stories about Target's great store experience and prices. This evolved tone and voice will strengthen the emotional bond we have with our guests while our circulars will continue to feature fewer items, more groceries and trip driving commodities, and a stronger emphasis on price and value."[15]

Target's outreach has been proved effective. In 2010, 53 percent of moms said they shopped at a Target retailer with a limited grocery section in the past three months (Walmart Supercenter had 59 percent penetration).[16] This value for quality clothing positioning is especially appealing to women, since 45 percent of moms said they would be willing to sacrifice the quality of clothes for themselves to get a better value in 2010.[17] Moms say Target allows them to get quality clothing without breaking the bank.

"Target has a really good selection of more inexpensive clothes. They are well made but really cute," Mickey, a mom of a middle schooler, elementary schoolchild, toddler, and infant, said. "They've done a good job of keeping things trendy or fashionable."

Target (continued)

In addition to the quality of their clothes and other products, moms have also responded to the entire shopping experience at Target as they feel that they can take their children along on the trip. "When we go to Target, it can be about all of us," Melissa, a mom of a middle schooler, said. "I can get a Starbucks, and we can walk around, and it can be more an experience than just shopping."

Target has created this experience not only through its merchandise, but also through careful product placement. In their stores, the "baby" section is at the very back of the store, so customers walk through the clothing departments, the home department, and the toy department to reach the children's section.

Target caters to busy moms by offering a one-stop shopping experience for their household needs in a trendy setting. It provides fashionable products at reasonable prices and creates a whole shopping experience for moms and their children. The combination of emotional connection with value offerings has helped Target succeed in attracting busy moms.

mas gifts bought at the store. Additionally, while she admits that she likes Victoria's Secret's products, she does not approve of its "racy" campaigns.

> There's so much sex in them. I mean, the boys, at least in our presence, turn off the Victoria Secret commercials. When they come on, they click to something else. They're pornographic. Who is made like that?

> ~ *Carlotta, mom of teenagers*

In a recent study of women who work, Scarborough Research found that when women have downtime, they are far from sedentary.[18] The top activities of choice are exercise and other physical activity. The image of the dowdy mother who doesn't pay attention to her appearance is passé.

Some companies are missing the mark for this with teen and middle school moms. A Toys "R" Us ad showing a mom in generic jeans and a white T-shirt got a thumbs-down from moms, while a State Farm Insurance ad depicting a woman in a business suit bending down to tie a child's shoe got a thumbs-up.

O, The Oprah Magazine, a favorite among moms, highlighted chic moms in one of its 2010 style features titled "7 New Ways to Wear Khakis." "Frumpy uniform for dress-down Fridays and running errands? Not this year," the article proclaimed. The layout includes a thirty-seven-year-old stay-at-home mother in tuxedo stripe khakis and a pair of wedge sandals. It also depicts a forty-four-year-old sales executive and mother of three-year-old twins who refers to khakis as "the bread and butter of the closet." [19]

Quantitatively, teen moms are above average on relating extremely well to an image of a professional working mom. They are the group with the strongest favorable response to this image. In addition, they also like a contemporary mom representation.[20]

Young Adults

When children become young adults, the fashion tables may turn. Mom may now turn to her daughter for fashion advice. Diane, the divorced mother of three grown children, looks to her daughter, age twenty-one, for style counsel. "Tiffany is a fashion plate," Diane said of her daughter. "I copy off her, actually. She has a good eye for what's cute." When it comes to shopping, Diane joins other moms in favoring J. C. Penney for its sales and store brands. A note of caution, however: a mom who dresses like her teenage or young adult daughter may result in a guest appearance on *What Not to Wear*. The Learning Channel's reality television show, popular with moms of all ages, shines a direct spotlight on women and image as it undertakes fashion intervention and leads one woman per episode through a style overhaul.

Several of the episodes have featured moms. Jessie, age fifty-two, did not earn any points for dressing in her thirty-four-year-old daughter's bold Texan style. Disa dressed age-inappropriately by raiding her tween daughter's closet for a midlife revival. Lisa, a one-time aspiring drag racer, was stuck in hoodies and T-shirts. "After having kids at a young age, Lisa gave up her dreams of being a racer and her style went into a permanent pit stop of oversized hoodies, T-shirts and camo," the show's Web site states.[21] Kimberly, the mother of triplets, was found on the bottom rung of her own priority ladder and needed to learn the value of taking care of herself.

However, this advice on image and fashion does flow in both directions.

Mom does not stop mothering when the child reaches young adulthood—and she often still sees herself reflected in her child. As Diane notes about her son, "I just want him to look nice when he coaches a game; he has his nice slacks on and a shirt tucked in with Sunday shoes."

Mom also has an opportunity to coach and counsel. As Irma notes, her twenty-one-year-old son will ask her what he should wear when he has an event or a special engagement to attend during the weekends. That counseling role may extend to young adult spouses as well:

> At times, my daughter-in-law will call me about clothing. Simple questions: "How do you think this would look on me?" With her, it's just her weight: "You know, I want to get this, but don't know if it will look good on me." She's very self-conscious about weight. She will call before she goes out shopping. There were a couple of time I told her—after she just had Mariana, her baby—that top will show your stomach a lot. She says "I know you'll be honest."
>
> ~ Isabel, mom of a young adult

We heard of moms providing guidance to their young adult child when the young adult wishes to portray a more mature image. Niki's perspective is typical:

> This year I did my own shopping. I had to get outfits for interviews and other things. I would always check with my mom from her perspective because I want to maintain a good image. And she will be super honest and say "that's too low-cut." I have a teenager perspective, and I want her perspective to look right.
>
> ~ Niki, a young adult

Conclusion

Moms of the twenty-first century are active and engaged. Their interest in fashion and beauty may change dramatically over the course of motherhood—guided by the mental, physical, and financial demands of raising children. It is important to note, however, that moms have definite opinions about what they and their children wear.

Moms of infants, toddlers, and preschoolers may feel tired and frumpy, but they do not necessarily want to be depicted as such. Over time, as children grow older, moms may recommit to themselves, making time for self-care. Stay-at-home moms may throw on stylish activewear for a fitness class and a stop at the local coffeehouse. Working moms, further along in their careers, may have more cash available for fashion and beauty. Moms of teenage girls may find their own sense of style recharged by daughters who are keenly interested in fashion. Moms of young adults may exchange fashion and appearance advice as a two-way dialogue with their Millennial children. This is a prime opportunity for brands to align with an evolving market.

Moms have a powerful voice when it comes to spending, and they are quick to name brands and organizations that they feel do a poor job depicting them and/or connecting with them. The flip side of this all-important coin is that companies that successfully recognize the desire of today's moms to be attractive and pulled-together will win their business. Toyota plays to this preference with its "diaper bag" Sienna van commercial. The mom behind the wheel is no plain Jane. She is a stylish, hip young mom who tells viewers, "People are shocked to find out I'm a mom. I hear 'hot babysitter' a lot." In a humorous play to moms—many of whom can relate to the experience—the woman's true identity is revealed when some police officers on the sidewalk point out a diaper bag she left on the van's roof.[22]

The way in which diaper-bag mom and others respond to marketing varies somewhat across subgroups; moms with three or more children, and those with infants and toddlers, relate more to the traditional and put-together stay-at-home marketing approach and image. Moms of preschoolers are most attracted to a marketing approach with a contemporary mom. Additionally, those with children ages thirteen to seventeen resonate with the professional working mom image. [23]

Moms in general are drawn to brands that deliver style at reduced prices, making stores like Target a top choice. Suave successfully addressed the mom market with a campaign that promised quality and model hair for model moms. Across the board, moms perceive that more companies targeted moms in 2009 than the year before (up from 91 percent to 98 percent).[24] Overall, 58 percent of moms felt that advertisements are effective in targeting them.[25]

Emotional appeal remains a strong draw for moms. Marketing approaches that appeal across subgroups are those that show a mom having fun with her kids (91 percent), make moms laugh (87 percent), acknowledge the multitasking life of moms (87 percent), and offer suggestions on ways to live healthier (84 percent).[26]

Fashion and Beauty

THEME RESOURCE GUIDE

	Mom's Concern For Her Child	Mom's Concern For Herself
Infant/Toddler Moms	• Comfort/move freely • Some individuality	• "Put together" aspirational, but low priority • Camouflage weight gain/ address weight gain
Preschool Moms	• Comfort/move freely • Some individuality	• Be contemporary • Camouflage weight gain/ address weight gain
Elementary School Moms	• Presentable for school • Sports affiliation	• Contemporary • Professional
Middle School Moms	• Emerging adult image – appropriate look	• Beginning of refocus on self
Moms of Teens	• Veto power – too low-cut	• Update image
Moms of Young Adults	• Coach child to dress as adult/ project right image in key situations (e.g., job interview)	• Keep contemporary

■ = Higher Mom's priority
■ = Moderate Mom's priority
□ = Lower Mom's priority

The Theme Resource Guide: Fashion and Beauty provides a quick synopsis of mom's fashion concerns for herself and child at different child age stages. For example, when looking at "Mom's Concerns for Herself" in this area, we see that mom puts a higher priority on updating her image as her child reaches the teen years, and then keeping contemporary during her child's young adult years. Another example from "Mom's Concern for Her Child" is where she may give her young adult child advice on the appropriate clothing to wear in a professional situation like a job interview.

While fashion and beauty may not be a top financial priority for many moms, significant opportunities exist for companies that pay careful attention to how moms view themselves and the images they choose to create for themselves. In addition, all brands can benefit from thinking about how mom wants to be portrayed in communications (e.g., as contemporary and up-to-date, not dowdy). There is an open market at the intersection of style and value.

Notes

1. Marketing to Moms Coalition, *State of the American Mom* 2010.
2. Ibid.
3. Ibid., 2009.
4. Chantal Todé, Direct Marketing News, "Suave Gives Its Marketing, and Consumers, a Makeover," March 7, 2005, accessed March 29, 2010, http://www.dmnews.com/suave-gives-its-marketing-and-consumers-a-makeover/article/86890/.
5. PR Newswire, "Can Motherhood and Womanhood Co-Exist?: New Report Reveals 77 Percent of Moms Don't Do Enough to Take Care of Themselves," accessed March 30, 2010, http://www.prnewswire.com/news-releases/canmotherhood-and-womanhood-co-exist-57889362.html.
6. Unilever, accessed March 30, 2010, http://www.unilever.ca/brands/personalcarebrands/suave.aspx.
7. Advertolog Advertising Archive, Suave Hair Products, "Mophead," April 2007, accessed May 19, 2011, http://www.advertolog.com/suave/print-outdoor/mophead-9637105/.
8. Personal interview with Marcelle Saporta, March 19, 2010.
9. Ibid.
10. Marketing to Moms Coalition, *State of the American Mom* 2010.

11. Ibid., 2009.

12. Ibid.

13. Ibid.

14. Target, "Fashion," accessed June 8, 2010, http://pressroom.target.com/
pr/news/fashion/default.aspx.

15. "Target Corporation Q1 2009 Earnings Call Transcript," accessed May
19, 2011, http://seekingalpha.com/article/138793-target-corporation-q1-
2009-earnings-call-transcript.

16. Marketing to Moms Coalition, *State of the American Mom* 2010.

17. Ibid.

18. Scarborough Research, "Multichannel Marketing: How to Reach the
Working Mom." accessed May 19, 2011, http://www.scarborough.com/
press_releases/Working%20Moms%20Free%20Study%20Version%20
FINAL%201.20.10.pdf.

19. Adam Glassman, "7 New Ways to Wear Khakis," *O, The Oprah Magazine,*
July 2010, accessed May 19, 2011, http://www.oprah.com/style/Womens-
Khakis-Summer-2010-Trends/1.

20. Marketing to Moms Coalition, *State of the American Mom* 2009.

21. TLC, *What Not to Wear,* http://tlc.discovery.com/fansites/whatnottowear/
episodes/season-7/episode-guide.html.

22. "Diaper Bag Commercial," accessed June 18, 2010, http://youtube.com/
watch?v=1i5MefpooUg.

23. Marketing to Moms Coalition, *State of the American Mom* 2009.

24. Ibid.

25. Ibid.

26. Ibid.

CHAPTER 8

Conclusion: Brand Sweet Spots and Actions

Too often we see brands pressured into approaches that are irrelevant and off-target to mom—from those that are overly broad to those that are overly familiar and presumptuous. How does one, as a brand leader or brand advisor, avoid such a fate?

As a strategic starting point, we recommend that brand leaders leverage the insights of mom's needs as articulated in this book to develop the most powerful branding, marketing, selling, product, and service experience approach for their brand. Specifically, we suggest using both (1) the age of oldest child mindset, as well as (2) the hot-button theme mindset. After analyzing both mindsets and their intersection, the brand leaders can make the selection best suited for their brand. In some cases, this selection will represent a hybrid of the two approaches. In other cases, one of the two mindsets may dominate the best branding approach. Either way, the level of insight and precision in the brand's marketing and targeting focus will result in more successful brand-building efforts instead of relying on generalized insights. We believe that it is critical for optimal success to take the time to approach brand development in this disciplined fashion.

The first lens for the brand is to consider which age of child group is most relevant for its products and services. In some cases, this age of child selection may seem clear and easy. For example, products for very young children are often focused on a specific developmental age of child, such as eighteen-month-old children. Toys are often organized in this fashion. We suggest taking the time to consider carefully. There may be an opportunity to attract new users, to capture additional usage occasions, and/or to displace substitute competitive brands. For example, our research finds that the iPhone is very popular among moms of toddlers. We see that Apple has successfully suggested to mom that her toddler can use the iPhone to learn and to be entertained. In this way, then, the iPhone may displace some of the traditional "toys" designed for eighteen-month-old children. However, this approach would not have worked if Apple had considered all moms as identical or assumed that the iPhone could not be used by a toddler. Another example of an age of child decision that requires more reflection is found in education: should a university, for instance, begin its brand outreach to moms prior to the junior and senior years of high school? If so, when should it begin (middle school, elementary school, etc.)? We find that mom is highly involved with her child's college selection process (a recent *Atlantic* article suggested this is particularly the case of moms of boys[1]), and ignoring her and focusing only on the high school junior or senior will miss a major market opportunity: influencer (and in many cases, funder). Another aspect to consider is whether your brand's focus in targeting mom is for her influence and direct spending on items for her child, or for items for herself and/or her household. Mom's role can be the primary or shared decision maker and purchasing agent, or the influencer or role model to her older child who is the primary decision maker for his or her own purchases.

Age of Child Lens

A summary and comparison organized according to the age of child lens follows. Each of the six child age ranges will be discussed, looking first at mom's concerns for her child and then at mom's concern for herself. This is intended to aid the reader who prefers to focus on the age of child lens rather than the hot-button theme lens.

Infants/Toddlers

The infant/toddler years are characterized by rapid child development through a series of milestones. Mom's concerns for her child are at their highest levels in first, food, and second, safety and health. Specifically, in the area of food, mom is most concerned with developing a broad taste palate for her child and providing good overall nutrition. Mom's health and safety concerns for her infant or toddler child center on physical safety and adult supervision. Two other areas hold moderate to lower priority for mom in the infant/toddler age ranges: education and exercise and sports. Mom's concerns for her child in the education area are primarily focused on gross motor skills development and cognitive stimulation. In the area of exercise and sports, the primary focus is physical activity and gross motor skills. While there can always be exceptions, two areas that are generally lower priority for mom's concerns for her child in these age ranges are fashion and beauty and technology.

In comparison, when a brand considers mom's concern for herself during her child's infant/toddler years, the two highest priority areas are first, food (specifically, weight management or loss), and second, technology (specifically, communicating with other adults and sharing, entertaining, and research). The areas that hold moderate priority when mom focuses on herself are exercise and sports (specifically, to get back in shape and get exercise) and education (specifically, some moms are pursuing degrees or certifications). Lower priority areas are safety and health, as well as fashion and beauty.

Looking across these themes, we see a common focus on food as a shared high-priority area, whether mom is thinking of her child or of herself. Two areas that share a moderate priority are education and exercise and sports (i.e., whether mom's concern for herself or mom's concern for her child). If a brand chooses to focus on the other three theme areas when targeting moms of infants/toddlers, it needs to recognize that the priority differs considerably between mom's concern for her child and mom's concern for herself. These other three areas are safety and health, fashion and beauty, and technology.

Preschoolers

The second age category is moms of preschoolers. The two highest priority areas of mom's concerns for her child continue to be food and safety and health. Within the food theme, the specific focus is on making sure her child develops healthy eating habits, and that her child's diet includes healthy foods, such as fruits and vegetables. The safety and health theme continues to emphasize physical safety and adult supervision for the children. The three areas of moderate priority are first, education (specifically, focus on gross motor skills, cognitive stimulation, socialization, and pre-kindergarten skills, such as colors); second, exercise and sports (specifically, keeping kids active and early sports involvement); and third, technology (specifically, education and entertainment). The lower priority area continues to be fashion and beauty, where mom's concerns for her child are mainly about her child's comfort and ability to move freely.

Looking at mom's concerns for herself, we see that the highest priority areas for the moms of preschoolers are technology and food, similar to moms of infants/toddlers. Moderate priority areas for these moms of preschoolers when it comes to themselves are education (specifically, some are getting degrees) and fitness (within exercise and sports). The area of fashion and beauty is also a moderate priority in this group. The lowest priority theme area for mom for herself is safety and health. Looking across the two approaches yields the insight that food is a shared high priority for mom for herself and for her child. Areas of shared moderate priority include technology (high for mom for herself, moderate for her child), exercise and sports (moderate for both), and education (moderate for both).

Elementary Schoolchildren

When it comes to mom's concerns for her child, moms of elementary schoolchildren have two different high-priority areas when compared with the younger age groups. The first high-priority theme is sports and exercise, where sports participation becomes an important part of the family lifestyle. The second high-priority theme is education, where academic building blocks like reading and writing are important. While safety and health is still a moderate priority, this is reduced from the high levels seen during the child's younger years. Similarly, food becomes only a moderate priority. Additionally, both fashion and beauty (with the need for her child to present himself or herself suitably at school) and technology (with a focus on education and entertainment) take on a moderate priority.

When focusing on herself, all but one of the areas (i.e., safety and health) are high or moderate priorities for moms of elementary schoolchildren. For example, mom uses technology even more for scheduling, mapping, and organizing her family's activities as extracurriculars become more prevalent at this age. For a brand that is targeting moms of elementary schoolchildren, then, there are a number of strong connecting points in the theme areas of both mom's concern for her child and for herself. Those connecting points present opportunities.

Middle Schoolers

Middle school moms are another group rich in connecting points. When looking at these moms, we see that education carries a high priority, followed by sports and exercise. Food and technology carry a moderate priority. Technology becomes a way for the child to check in with mom as many children get a cell phone at this age range. Related to technology, cyber safety pops up as a safety concern at a moderate level, as does sports safety. In the area of fashion and beauty, mom has a moderate priority concern with making sure her child is wearing age-appropriate clothing that fits the child's adolescent figure.

When looking at mom's concern for herself, we can see that moms of middle schoolers begin to refocus more on themselves, as seen through the higher priority that they place on fashion and beauty. In the technology area, the cell phone becomes the lifeline to her child and is a moderately high priority. Other areas of high priority for mom's concern for herself during her child's middle school years are exercise and sports and food. The safety and health area continues to be a lower priority for herself. While some moms in this range will focus on education for themselves, this priority is moderate to low. The comparison of these themes highlights a number of connecting point opportunities, as well as the convergence in the technology area of the cell phone.

Teenagers

During the teenage years, identifying the areas of opportunity requires a careful examination as well as creativity. The highest priority for mom's concerns for her child during the teen years are safety and health (specifically, teen driving and concerns with the areas of alcohol, drug use, and safe sex). In fact, a recent study by the Substance Abuse and Mental Health Services Administration (SAMHSA) found that a small number of parents (6 percent) are introducing their children to alcohol during middle school.[2] Some moms are concluding that they would rather introduce their child to alcohol in the home environment versus allowing the introduction to happen in a less controlled environment. Also in the teenage years, education for her child is a high priority for mom, with attention placed on getting a college education and/or an occupationally relevant education. During these years, technology continues to be a moderate priority, as does encouraging healthy on-the-go food choices. The exercise and sports area priority is mixed—high if the child plays high school sports, otherwise low. The fashion and beauty area receives a lower priority.

When looking at mom's concern for herself during her child's teenage years, we find that several areas carry a high priority for mom, including food, exercise and sports, safety and health, fashion and beauty, and technology. In general, education has a lower priority for mom for herself during these years.

Young Adults

During the young adult years, mom's two highest priority concerns for her child are education (specifically, career and job choices) and technology. Fashion and beauty is also a moderately high priority with mom coaching her child on how to project the right image in certain situations through clothing choices. There are also three lower priority areas of mom's concerns for her child: food, exercise and sports, and safety and health. While these areas are less important at the young adult age, mom is still called upon to provide advice on an on-call, as-needed basis.

During her child's young adult years, mom's concerns for herself are found at fairly high levels in several areas, similar to the teenage years. The strongest areas of overlap between mom's concerns for her child and mom's concerns for herself are found in fashion and beauty and technology.

Hot-Button Theme Lens

The second lens for the brand is to assess or examine which hot-button theme(s) to align with and why. By aligning with mom's hot-button areas, a brand or organization will increase its chance of engaging mom and getting her to "open her ears" to its offering. If the brand experience reaches her through one of her hot-buttons, she is more likely to tune in and to take the next step toward brand purchase or loyalty. Mom's hot-button themes of food, exercise and sports, safety and health, education, fashion and beauty, and technology all present opportunity. For each theme, the focus varies by age of child, and whether the focus is greater for mom for herself, for mom for her child, or shared by both.

Summary Example of a Hot-Button Theme: Exercise and Sports

The theme area of exercise and sports provides a good illustration of differing focus and levels of commitment by age of child, and the need for a brand to tailor its approach accordingly. When mom's child is an infant/toddler, there is only moderate to low interest around the topic of exercise for the child; mom typically perceives that her young child gets plenty of exercise in the course of learning new skills such as crawling, standing, walking, and using riding toys, for example. Additionally, mom's interest in sports for her child at these young age ranges is typically also low. Of greater interest and concern for the mom of an infant/toddler is typically her own exercise, as mom often gains weight during pregnancy that she is concerned with losing. An example of a brand that has addressed this mom concern is LUNA Mom's Club, powered by Stroller Strides. LUNA has tapped into the exercise hot-button area and aligned its brand through sponsorship with Stroller Strides.

By comparison, the preschool years represent a transition time in terms of the sports and exercise focus for mom and her child, with many moms continuing to focus on exercise for themselves, and to begin to focus on introducing their children to a selected preschool sport or sports.

At the elementary school level, sports rise in prominence for many moms, often shaping the family lifestyle around attending games on the weekends and practices during the week. At this point, mom's focus on her child getting exercise is typically less, because in-school physical education programs are generally part of her elementary schoolchild's normal routine. Instead, in the elementary school years, mom will often encourage her child to try different sports options in order to find a good fit.

While a subset of moms continue to have children who are highly involved with sports in middle school and high school, there is typically a drop-off in sports involvement for the balance of moms as other interests become more prominent for their children.

By young adulthood, very few adult children play organized sports, and mom's focus shifts back to a concern that her child is getting sufficient exercise. Mom will encourage her young adult to exercise through a variety of methods, including role modeling and exercising with the child when possible; researching and suggesting options that may hold appeal to her child based on her knowledge of the child's interests; and even purchasing a gym membership for the child. This presents another opportunity for brands or products that support mom.

We have included this brief summary of the exercise and sports theme by age of child to give the reader a sense of how these hot-button areas morph by age of child. This is not intended to replace the more complete, thorough discussion found in the individual chapter on exercise and sports. Additionally, since the preceding individual chapters outline the hot-button theme areas by age of child, we suggest that the reader refer to those individual chapters for more detail on each theme (i.e., food, exercise and sports (complete explanation), education, safety and health, technology, and fashion and beauty). To make it easier for a brand or organization to focus its marketing efforts to moms using these insights, we have also provided a few tools. These tools, the Theme Resource Guides, are not meant to replace thoughtful evaluation, but can instead serve as a starting point. These Theme Resource Guides can be found at the end of each chapter as well as in this conclusion chapter.

Tools for Brand Leaders

The first such tool is the Theme Resource Guide: Mom's Concern for Her Child. This guide is organized by the themes covered in this work (i.e., food, exercise and sports, education, safety and health, technology, and fashion and beauty). The guide is designed to allow a marketer to quickly identify the age range for which the theme is identified as a priority. So, for example, if you look at the Theme Resource Guide: Mom's Concern for Her Child version, the hot-button theme of food column and the infant/toddler mom row, you will see this theme is more darkly shaded, indicating high importance. Additionally, the text gives a brief description of mom's overall focus; in this case, her priority is placed on her child's good overall nutrition and developing a broad taste palate. In reviewing the food column in the same guide further, you will see that for elementary school moms, the food theme has a medium shading, indicating a moderate priority. Specific focus areas for elementary school moms include "healthy" foods, especially fruits and vegetables, and fuel for sports. Scanning down the food column reveals that moms of young adults find food as a theme for their children as a relatively low priority. Thus, the shading is light for the lower priority. Our research found that while moms of young adults do influence their adult children's food choices, their influence is more on an on-call basis. Thus, the Theme Resource Guides work as a starting point in evaluating the intersection of a brand and targeted mom segments.

The second tool, similar to the first, is the Theme Resource Guide: Mom's Concern for Herself version. This tool is primarily intended to be used by brands that offer products mom will buy for herself, not for her children. Looking at the fashion and beauty column in the "Mom's Concern for Herself" version reveals differences in mom focus according to the age of her child. For example, for several moms, particularly those with younger children, fashion and beauty is an area that they give a lower priority for them-

Mom's Concern for Her Child

THEME RESOURCE GUIDE

	Food	Exercise and Sports	Education	Safety and Health	Technology	Fashion and Beauty
Infant/Toddler Moms	• Good overall nutrition and developing broad taste palate	• Sports not a focus • Exercise by moving around	• Gross motor skills and cognitive stimulation	• Physical safety • Adult supervision	• Entertainment (e.g., iPhone)	• Comfort/move freely • Some individuality
Preschool Moms	• "Healthy," fruits and vegetables, avoid excess sugar	• Keeping kid active • Sports starting	• Gross motor skills and cognitive stimulation • Socialization • Pre-K skills – colors, shapes	• Physical safety • Adult supervision	• Entertainment • Education	• Comfort/move freely • Some individuality
Elementary School Moms	• "Healthy," fruits and vegetables • Fuel for the day	• Sports participation family lifestyle	• Adjustment to classroom • Academic building blocks	• Playground/sports safety • Stranger danger	• Entertainment • Education	• Presentable for school • Sports affiliation
Middle School Moms	• Dinner focus • Encourage healthy choices	• Sports focus	• Academic foundation • Getting good grades	• Cyber safety • Sports safety	• Entertainment • Check in with mom	• Emerging adult image – appropriate look
Moms of Teens	• Encourage healthy on-the-go choices	• Depends on whether child plays sports	• Getting good grades • College • Scholarship	• Teen driving, drinking, drugs, sex ed	• Check in with mom • Entertainment	• Veto power – too low-cut
Moms of Young Adults	• Recipe and cooking advice • Guidance on better choices	• More concerns with adult child's exercise but little ability to impact	• Career/job results from education • Making good choices	• Some concerns around driving • Health insurance coverage	• Lifeline between parent and child	• Coach child to dress as adult/project right image in key situations (e.g., job interview)

■ = Higher Mom's priority
■ = Moderate Mom's priority
□ = Lower Mom's priority

selves. Additionally, we know that mom is more willing to sacrifice the quality of her own clothing than that of her child's clothing.[3] Additionally, while a contemporary image is appealing to moms across the child age segments, there is a desire for increased professionalism at the elementary school age range while the moms of teens are looking to refresh or update their image.[4]

It is suggested that both Theme Resource Guides be examined, as they each may suggest opportunities for your organization's brand. The two guides are meant to provide two different lenses for consideration within the framework of age of oldest child and hot-button theme. The goal is to look for intersections or "sweet spots" with which your brand can align, as we will discuss next.

After deciding on one or more "sweet spots" using the age of child and hot-button themes, the next step is to apply this insight to your organization's brand. Your organization's brand will need to identify the specific approach that you will take to align your brand either indirectly or directly with the chosen sweet spot. Through this research and our experience, we have identified four proven ways to go about this. Undoubtedly, there are more approaches available, and so these four options are intended only to get you started. In addition, the approaches can be combined. These four approaches are (1) case example application; (2) checking in with moms online and in person; (3) holding a professional brainstorming session around benefit areas and generating a broad range of ideas to test with moms; and (4) looking for relevant partnerships.

Case Example Application

The first approach is to examine case examples from the brands in this book. We suggest identifying additional case study brands that hold interest and relevancy for your organization, and which will be used for inspiration. The key in selecting case studies is to identify brands that have been successful with the target age group and/or theme interest. We recommend identifying no more than three case examples in total. Once you have selected the case studies, the process begins by diving deep within the selected brands by interviewing their management, reviewing their branding materials, gathering any publicly available data, and searching for moms' online comments about the brand. Next, it is important to take the time to distill the case example and to go through it in detail with your organization's brand leadership team. In exploring the case example, it is critical to take the time to capture the benefits and features that the case study brand offers. After

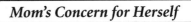

Mom's Concern for Herself

THEME RESOURCE GUIDE

	Food	Exercise and Sports	Education	Safety and Health	Technology	Fashion and Beauty
Infant/Toddler Moms	• Weight management or loss	• Exercise • Get back in shape	• Some are getting degrees	• No strong concerns	• Communicate with adults • Share entertain, research	• "Put together" aspirational, but low priority • Camouflage weight gain/address weight gain
Preschool Moms	• Weight management or loss	• Exercise and fitness	• Some are getting degrees	• No strong concerns	• Communicate with adults • Share, entertain, research	• Be contemporary • Camouflage weight gain/address weight gain
Elementary School Moms	• Weight management	• Exercise and fitness	• Some are getting degrees	• No strong concerns	• Scheduling, mapping, organizing	• Contemporary • Professional
Middle School Moms	• Weight management	• Exercise and fitness • Weight management	• Some are getting degrees	• No strong concerns	• Lifeline to child starts	• Beginning of refocus on self
Moms of Teens	• Weight management	• Exercise for health	• Less involved for self	• Disease prevention/control	• Lifeline to child continues	• Update image
Moms of Young Adults	• Weight management	• Exercise for health	• Less involved for self	• Disease prevention/control	• Lifeline to child continues	• Keep contemporary

■ = Higher Mom's priority
■ = Moderate Mom's priority
▨ = Lower Mom's priority

these benefits and features are identified, the next step is to build an analogy by asking how these features and benefits could apply to your own brand. Clearly, a fresh application is a key to success, and it goes without saying that we recommend avoiding literal copying the other brand.

Check In with Moms

The second approach is to talk with moms who have children in the relevant age range about one's brand and about the theme(s). There are many appropriate qualitative and quantitative approaches including, but not limited to, interviews, ethnographic observations, blogging, quantitative online surveys, and focus groups either online, in home, or at a professional focus group facility. Some organizations also set up an ongoing panel of "advisory" moms who can provide feedback for the organization's brand. The benefit of this advisory group is that that they may be more available for ad hoc examination and ongoing consultation. Clearly, there is no substitute for the direct involvement of the organization's brand team in conjunction with these moms to develop a "gut feel" for the consumer as compared with an exclusively cerebral approach. Since this book is not intended as a market research primer, we suggest consulting with a market research professional, as needed, for expertise in how to design and conduct the research.

Hold a Professional Brainstorming Session

A professionally led brainstorming session is a third approach. In our experience, this is a good investment to ensure a wide range of initial ideas and to tap into different sources for creatively aligning the brand. In the brainstorming session, we suggest including a good mix of creative thinkers—preferably from different parts of the organization. We recommend you think broadly about whom to include, as sometimes the most creative thinkers can be found in surprising functions—such as a credit officer in a bank or an actuary in an insurance company—not just in the product development or marketing functional areas. The goal is to ensure a range of ideas to develop alignment and consider several options. Of note, it can also be helpful to include moms in the session, or to hold a separate session with moms. A professional facilitator will ensure your time is well spent, that you use best practice approaches, and that your session is structured to achieve your goals.

Look for Relevant Partnerships

The fourth approach we suggest is to look for relevant partnerships. The LUNA partnership with Stroller Strides, and the Sara Lee Soft & Smooth partnership with Disney's *High School Musical* are two examples discussed in this book. We also suggest the brand take the time to consider ongoing, meaningful partnerships, rather than trying to do a number of smaller, less impactful initiatives.

There are many other approaches to developing branding tactics and strategies after selecting the age of child and theme area. However, these four can serve as a good starting point when embarking upon the journey of capturing mom's purchasing and brand loyalty. We hope that you find the discovery process is productive and "bears fruit" for your brand.

Looking ahead, we also believe that there is more to be learned in the ongoing influence of mom with her adult children. Specifically, we suggest looking at mom's influence on adult children beyond the age of twenty-nine, where our research ended. This area could be particularly interesting to study by following the current young adult cohort as they move into their thirties, forties, and fifties. We hypothesize that the close relationships and frequent communication between today's young adults and their moms will lead to a greater impact of mom's influence on her middle-aged adult child's life.

Also outside the scope of this work is the impact of grandmothers and a specific focus on moms with children who have special needs. These two areas are receiving attention currently, while to our knowledge, the topic of mom's impact on children above the age of thirty is less explored. Additionally, we are aware that there is interest in better understanding the impact of dads as well as mom/dad joint decision making. While these topics are interesting, our intent was to focus on moms and to offer insights for brands and organizations that recognize that mom herself is the primary or head decision maker for their brand.

We wish you great success in tuning into mom!

Notes

1. Hanna Rosin, *The Atlantic*, "The End of Men," July/August 2010, accessed June 30, 2010, http://www.theatlantic.com/magazine/archive/2010/07/the-end-of-men/8135.

2. Melinda Beck, "Dad, I Prefer the Shiraz: Do Parents Who Serve Teens Beer and Wine at Home Raise Responsible Drinkers?" March 8, 2011, accessed [insert date you accessed this article], http://online.wsj.com/article/SB10001424052748703386704576186380879004132.html.
3. Marketing to Moms Coalition, State of the American Mom 2010.
4. Ibid., 2009.

APPENDIX

We utilized several research methods to build a solid understanding of moms by age of segment that is both broad in scope and rigorous in analysis. In particular, this book cites four major resources:

1. *State of the American Mom* quantitative reports (2007, 2008, 2009, and 2010)

2. Due-diligence review of existing research

3. In-depth, qualitative interviews with moms

4. Case study research

The methodological and analytical techniques of each resource are articulated below.

State of the American Mom *Quantitative Research*

The *State of the American Mom* (*SOAM*) report was first distributed in 2007 by the Marketing to Moms Coalition, an independent, nonprofit organization dedicated to supporting and promoting an understanding of mothers as the most powerful consumer group in the United States. The Coalition's mission is to provide actionable data and insights on American moms to retailers, manufacturers, and other professionals that market to moms, as well as to provide a benchmark for ongoing tracking of trends.

The surveys were fielded in the beginning of the third quarters of 2007, 2008, and 2009, and in the second quarter of 2010. The 2009 and 2010 surveys were made possible through the gracious sponsorship of Current Lifestyle Marketing and Weber Shandwick.

Online Panel: Quantitative Sample and Fielding

Each year the Coalition uses a third-party mail panel provider to contact a nationally representative sample of American moms via online invitation. In a span of four years, over 4,800 moms with children under eighteen living at home completed the online questionnaire (2007, 2008, 2009, and 2010). This resulted in an ending sample of 1,279 moms in 2007; 1,033 in 2008; 1,225 in 2009; and 1,273 in 2010. Within this total group, a Spanish-speaking sample of 200 moms also completed the survey in 2008, 2009, and 2010. The decision to include a sample of Spanish-speaking moms was motivated by a growing interest in the Hispanic market and the shifting demographics of American mothers. According to the Pew Research Center, in 2008 the share of births to white females was considerably lower at 53 percent when compared with 65 percent in 1990. On the other hand, the number of births to Hispanic mothers has been growing and is expected to continue due to higher birthrates and immigration.[1] As a result, Hispanics are deliberately overrepresented in the sample due to the additional Spanish-speaking group along with an English-speaking Hispanic group. In addition to Hispanics, the work also included a sample of over one hundred African American moms each year. Other key demographic factors, such as household size and income, were balanced to ensure a representative fact base.

MarketTools (the third-party mail panel provider) used their own online panel comprised of more than two million people to invite moms to participate. A link was sent to qualifying individuals via an online invitation that specified the security and anonymity of the survey and informed the reader of the survey's purpose. Participants took the survey using a secure Web site and received points in return for their responses. These points could then be redeemed for goods such as electronics, music, cookware, and more.[2]

In addition to ensuring the quantity of responses, MarketTools also ensures the quality of the survey respondents. MarketTools uses a proprietary data quality technology called TrueSample to eliminate low-quality respondents. TrueSample validates the survey respondents at the panel level and the survey level to catch false, duplicate, or unengaged respondents. The company also uses an automated technology to verify the respondents' identities. This filter secures the quality and validity of the survey results.[3]

Survey Design

After reading through an introduction, participants completed the survey, which was designed to be clear, accessible, and readable. Questions included

FIGURE 9.1. *STATE OF THE AMERICAN MOM* SURVEY BREAKDOWN COMPARED TO CENSUS ESTIMATES OF MOMS WITH CHILDREN UNDER EIGHTEEN.

	Moms with Children under 18	Marketing to Moms Survey Sample
Caucasian	60%	58%
Hispanic*	19%	25%
Black	13%	15%
Asian	5%	2%

	Moms with Children under 18	Marketing to Moms Survey Sample
Under $35,000	34%	36%
$35,000 - $75,000	32%	40%
$75,000+	34%	25%

	Moms with Children under 18	Marketing to Moms Survey Sample
Moms with only one child	43%	42%
Moms with 2 children	36%	36%
Moms 3+ children	20%	22%

Source: U.S. Census Bureau (November 2009). *Current Population Survey* State of the American Mom (2009), Marketing to Moms Coalition

a variety of formats—including a combination of closed and open-ended questions—to best capture the participants' opinions. The surveys were designed to take approximately twenty-five to forty minutes, but moms were allowed to set their own pace. No time limit was enforced. Each participant was allowed only one submission.

Because this was done on a voluntary and nationwide scale, in-house surveying or physical materials were not used to survey participants. The individual needed access to a computer and Internet connection (not provided by the Coalition or MarketTools) in order to participate in the survey.

The surveys were designed by Insight to Action and the Coalition. They consisted of a variety of data-rich questions and response choices. The major areas covered in the survey included:

There were a total of thirty-four (2007), sixty-six (2008), ninety (2009), and seventy-four (2010) questions in the four versions of the survey. The surveys were modified from year to year to account for emerging trends (highlighted in gray). For example, in 2009 a section on family economics was included to assess the impact of the recession. Likewise, a growing interest in health and fitness in 2010, social networking in 2009, and environmental concerns in 2008 prompted the incorporation of these sections into the survey.

Analysis and Evaluation

Upon receipt of the survey results, Insight to Action, Inc. analyzed the data in a secure fashion and created reports that detailed the number of respondents per question and possible response (for instance, in the 2010 survey, 497 mothers listed themselves as employed "full time"). Furthermore, Insight to Action analyzed moms by a variety of factors, such as age of child, number of child(ren), ethnicity, and household income. This detailed analysis yielded a rich understanding of the differences and similarities among moms and their attitudes toward certain topics. The data was combined with other aspects of the *SOAM* study to provide a comprehensive view of how mothers choose to make purchasing decisions.

Most data included in this book looks at responses of moms by age of child, particularly the oldest child. Age of the oldest child was the most discriminating factor in understanding mom's perspective on a range of issues compared with other demographic factors analyzed, such as working status, marital status, gender of child, ethnicity, and household income. As a result, we have structured our book not only by topic, but also by the age of the oldest child. We believe this provides the richest responses and most

FIGURE 9.2. *SOAM* OVERVIEW.

2007	2008	2009
1. Introduction and Purpose	1. Introduction and Purpose	1. Introduction and Purpose
2. Methodology and Sample	2. Methodology and Sample	2. Methodology and Sample
3. The Most Important Priorities	3. Juggling Family Life Demands	3. Moms' Priorities and Schedules
4. Juggling Family Life Demands	4. Keeping Connected	4. Family Economics
5. Busy Kids/Busy Mom	5. The Most Important Priorities	5. Environmental Engagement
6. Money and Kid's Allowances	6. "Green" Interest	6. Marketing Impressions/Impact
7. The Cellphone Lifeline	7. Marketing Impressions/Impact	7. Shopping Tendancies and Child Influence
8. Kid Influences on Household Purchase Decisions	8. Shopping and Retail Tendancies	8. Food and Nutrition
9. Demographics	9. Kid Influences on Household Purchase Decisions	9. Information Sources
	10. Demographics	10. Media Habits
		11. Social Networking
		12. Keeping Connected
		13. Demographics

Source: State of the American Mom 2009, Marketing to Moms Coalition

insightful analysis to help marketers understand and make themselves relevant to moms. As deemed appropriate, we might selectively include other demographic groups to provide an added layer of focus. For instance, in looking at the major themes of food, we found it helpful to examine the differences between the moms of preschool children who were working outside of the home as compared with those who were not working outside the home. In this case, notable differences emerged in preschool child influence on moms' food choices.

The findings from these surveys are included throughout the book to provide a full perspective of the mom market.

Due Diligence of Existing Research

Throughout the project, we also reviewed existing research on marketing to moms and relevant national trends. The three primary uses for this research were to 1) determine demographic breakdowns of the total mom population and its total spending; 2) identify topics of interest and macro trends such as health or safety issues; and 3) obtain an "on-the-ground" perspective from newspapers, business journals, and social media outlets.

Demographic data was the starting point of our analysis as it helped us balance our sample in the quantitative survey and qualitative interviews. Moreover, it helped us estimate the size of the mom market, as well as its total spending. In order to obtain this information, we utilized the Current Population Survey and the Consumer Expenditure Survey from the U.S. Census Bureau.

It is important to recognize that mom's purchase influence reaches beyond her direct buys. Our experience working with young adults in the financial service and education markets gave us impetus to examine this influence area. We found that many young adults continue to consult their moms on purchase decisions and consider them one of their most trusted resources even after leaving home. As a result, we decided to include moms of young adults in our research.

Including moms of young adults in our research required us to define and estimate their impact since there is less existing research in this area. Our definition of young adult is ages eighteen to twenty-nine. We arrived at this definition by leveraging years of experience in financial services and education. Since Census data does not track moms with children over eighteen years old, we took the next step to quantify the market size. Therefore, in order to calculate the percent of total moms with children eighteen to twenty-nine, we utilized the Current Population Survey data from November 2009 and November 1999. In 1999, 26.7 million moms had children ages six to seventeen, and essentially this same number of moms would have children ages sixteen to twenty-seven in 2009. Using this as our gauge, we calculated the ratio of moms with children ages sixteen to twenty-seven to the total adult population of sixteen- to twenty-seven-year-olds. Assuming that the same ratio is relatively accurate for moms of eighteen- to twenty-nine-year-olds, we were able to estimate that there are approximately 26.5 million moms with children eighteen to twenty-nine in 2009. Since there are forty-nine million young adults ages eighteen to twenty-nine in the United States, this estimate appears reasonable. Other mom groups of interest were equally sizable: there are nine million moms with children ages zero to two, ten million moms with children ages three to five, twenty million moms with children ages six to thirteen, and twelve million moms with children ages fourteen to seventeen.[4]

FIGURE 9.3. U.S. MOM POPULATION BY AGE OF CHILDREN.

	Total
0-2	9,158,491
3-5	9,531,671
6-13	20,339,859
14-17	11,893,826
18-29	26,500,672
Total Moms	77,428,180

Source: U.S. Census Bureau (November 2009 and November 1999). *Current Population Survey,* ITA Moms of Young Adults Analysis (January 2010)

Furthermore, we leveraged government data to calculate the dollar market size in terms of purchasing power of groups of moms by age of child. Currently, it is estimated that moms control 85 percent of U.S. household purchases and spend $2.4 trillion annually.[5] Using the Consumer Expenditure Survey, we were able to further quantify the potential of the mom market by age of child. Among married households, moms with an oldest child under six account for an estimated $345 billion; moms with an oldest child age six to seventeen drive $1,137 billion; and moms with an oldest child eighteen years and older are in charge of spending $697 billion annually. Not to mention that single moms with children under seventeen years old control an additional $270 billion. This information helps validate the importance of the mom market and why it should be a significant focus for marketers.[6]

FIGURE 9.4. MOM MARKET BY AGE OF CHILD.

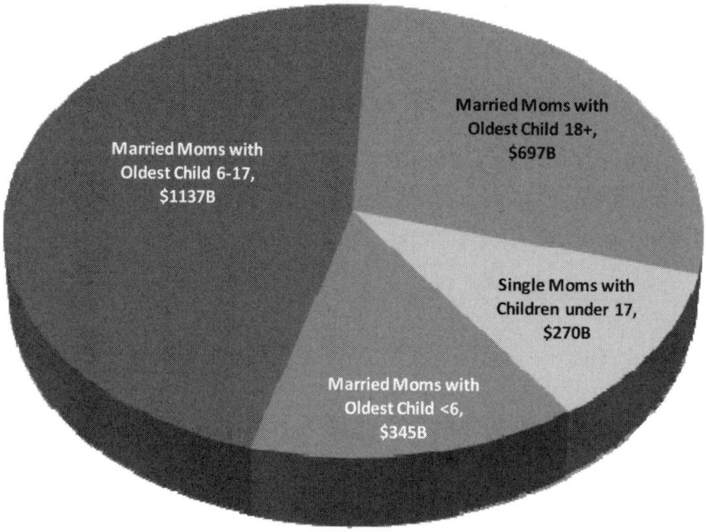

Source: Bureau of Labor Statistics (2008).   *Consumer Expenditure Survey*

In addition to the population and market size estimates, we also conducted a review of secondary information offered by governmental agencies such as the Centers for Disease Control and Prevention. These sources were valuable in identifying macro trends related to moms within the United States and topics of interest, including demographic changes and health concerns. Along with the primary research inputs, these macro trends helped us hone in on the areas that are important to moms and marketers, which gave our analysis a focus grounded in current trends.

After identifying macro trends, we relied on qualitative information from newspapers, business journals, and social media outlets to make the findings more robust and to add an "on-the-ground" perspective to the data. As a result, we saw the story behind the numbers presented both in the national findings and in our quantitative research. For example, we used mom and parenting blogs to determine what real moms were saying about the products. Many of our case studies and chapters include blog comments from moms who posted statements relevant to the topic at hand. These comments enriched our understanding of moms' reactions to certain products and trends—an understanding that would not be available based solely on quantitative data.

In-Depth Qualitative Interviews

We also individually interviewed twenty-four moms with children ages zero to twenty-nine. Participants were recruited via a large network of family and friends. These moms were selected to be representative across a variety of factors, including age of children, race, ethnicity, and marital status. Most of the interviews were conducted in English and lasted between forty-five and ninety minutes.

Figure 9.5 depicts a sample breakdown.[7]

Interview Design

The qualitative interview was broken out into two major phases. Phase I interviews were conducted early in the process and, therefore, were broader in scope. Phase II interviews were conducted after the themes had been identified and, as a result, followed a more focused interview format.

In Phase I, ten moms were interviewed and asked to share their thoughts and opinions on a range of issues, including their priorities, concerns, and brands they thought had taken an innovative approach to marketing or had helped them in their role as a mom. The goal was to understand broadly what engages moms at different child age ranges and how this influences their thinking around brands and their messages. Coupled with the quantitative data, the perspective of Phase I moms helped us identify and refine the themes on which to focus.

Phase II was conducted after the six themes had been defined. The themes that emerged are food, exercise and sports, education, safety and health, technology, and fashion and beauty. As a result, these interviews were more focused, with fourteen moms asked to describe their experiences

FIGURE 9.5. *STATE OF THE AMERICAN MOM* SURVEY BREAKDOWN COMPARED TO US CENSUS TOTAL MOM POPULATION (INCLUDES CHILDREN OVER 18).

	% of Total Moms (Census Data)	% of Qualitative Interviews
Marital Status		
Married	79%	70%
Single	9%	9%
Widowed/Divorced/Separated	12%	22%
Household Income		
Under 35,000	32%	30%
35K-75K	35%	30%
75K+	34%	35%
Ethnicity*		
Caucasian	68%	65%
African American	11%	9%
Hispanic *	14%	22%
Asian	5%	4%

Source: U.S. Census Bureau (November 2009 and November 1999).
Current Population Survey

and candidly share their opinions on each of the six key topics explored in this book, as well as any related parenting concerns and/or brands that had helped them.

In both phases the interviews were intended to be informal, which allowed the moms to speak freely about their experiences and gave us the flexibility to focus on what was important to each of the participants. Not surprisingly, certain areas were less relevant to moms of certain child age groups. For example, sports was a greater focus for moms of elementary school children, while exercise was most relevant to moms of the youngest and oldest children.

In total, we completed twenty-four interviews; their narratives were designed to provide a more comprehensive look into the emotions, needs, and decision-making processes of moms.

Analysis and Evaluation

Excerpts from these interviews have been used where appropriate in the chapters, as they add insights from the "frontline" on many of the trends and topics explored in this book. Rather than relying solely on data, we use these moms' stories as concrete examples that corroborate the trend data available from the quantitative fact base and the secondary resources.

Case Study Research

Throughout the book, we have included real-world examples of companies that have successfully positioned themselves to appeal to mothers. These case studies are classified in their respective chapters based on the topics covered. Additionally, the case studies also are classified according to the age of children since we have determined that focusing on the age of oldest child yields the greatest insight into moms' attitudes and behaviors. These classifications are meant to be directional rather than absolute.

The examples help provide real-world lessons that brands and organizations can use to create strategies and products that reach moms, a crucial segment in the American marketplace. We leveraged our expert knowledge of the market and what we learned from *real* moms to identify case study candidates. We assessed these candidates based on access to information, and we noted recognition in marketing to moms.

To develop these case studies, we identified articles and news releases that contained information about the company's actions. These articles helped us obtain the information necessary to flesh out the driving forces behind the brand's approach. When we relied on the company's own corporate communications for these case studies, we also included information from mainstream media in order to offer a balanced perspective of the company's actions and results.

In addition, we interviewed select industry leaders and experts who shared with us their knowledge and experience of successful marketing approaches or products targeting moms. These interviews helped us understand the motivations behind certain companies' decisions.

FIGURE 9.6. TOPICS.

Topics	Case Studies	Age Group Relevancy
Education	1. Leapfrog	⇒ Infant/Toddler/Preschool Moms
	2. Purdue University	⇒ Moms of Young Adults
Health & Safety	3. Mrs. Meyers Clean Day	⇒ Infant/Toddler Moms
	4. State Farm Steer Clear	⇒ Moms of Young Adults/Teens
	5. Tonik	⇒ Moms of Young Adults
Food	6. Sara Lee Soft & Smooth	⇒ Preschool Moms
	7. Barilla Plus	⇒ Middle School Moms
Sports & Exercise	8. Luna	⇒ Infant/Toddler Moms
	9. Frosted Flakes	⇒ Middle School Moms
	10. NikeiD	⇒ Moms of Teens
Technology	11. iPhone	⇒ Infant/Toddler Moms
	12. Educational Products, Inc.	⇒ Elementary Moms
	13. Beatles Rock Band	⇒ Middle School Moms
	14. Skype	⇒ Moms of Young Adults
Fashion & Appearance	15. Suave	⇒ All Ages
	16. Target	⇒ All Ages

This synthesis of primary and secondary research techniques helped us obtain a wider variety of case studies, as we were able to rely both on internal contacts and published information. Moreover, the synthesis of these two approaches offered a balanced perspective on the companies' business situations.

Conclusion

This book provides marketers with a strong understanding of how they can tap into the significant mom market. The synthesis of these four different research methods provides a system of checks and balances to ensure quality insights as well as enhances the depth of these findings and, more importantly, their richness for marketers.

Notes

1. Gretchen Livingston and D'Vera Cohn, "The New Demography of American Motherhood," Pew Research Center, May 6, 2010, accessed May 15, 2011, http://pewresearch.org/pubs/1586/changing-demographic-characteristics-american-mothers.
2. Survey Blogger, "MarketTools ZoomPanel Research Panel US," January 26, 2009, accessed May 15, 2011, http://www.topfreesurvey.com/market-tools-zoompanel-research-panel-us/.
3. MarketTools TrueSample, accessed May 15, 2011, http://www.market-tools.com/sites/default/files/resources/data_sheet/DS_TrueSample.pdf.
4. U.S. Census Bureau (November 2009 and November 1999). Current Population Survey. The U.S Census Bureau does not track moms of eighteen- to twenty-nine-year-olds. To arrive at this estimate we leveraged Census data from November 1999.
5. Maria T. Bailey, *Power Moms: The New Rules for Engaging Mom Influencers Who Drive Brand Choice*, Wyatt-MacKenzie Publishing, Inc., 2011, 13.
6. Bureau of Labor Statistics (2010). Consumer Expenditure Survey.
7. U.S. Census Bureau (November 2009 and November 1999), Current Population Survey. The U.S. Census Bureau does not list "Hispanic" as a race. These numbers represent the total proportion of moms who chose

that race and listed themselves as being "Non-Hispanic" on a separate question about Hispanic origin. The U.S. Census Bureau also does not track moms of eighteen- to twenty-nine-year-olds. To arrive at this estimate we leveraged Census data from November 1999.

INDEX

athletes, athletics *(continued)* mentors in, 66; teens as, 49. *See also* sports and sportsmanship

baby, babies: bottles and bottle-feeding of, 14, 81–82; car seats for, 79, 81–83, 88; education and, 59–60; impact of, on moms, 127–29; nutrition and, 11–15; products for, 84–85; strollers and, 39. *See also* infants/toddlers

Barilla/Barilla PLUS, 31; case study of, 24–26

The Beatles Rock Band, 124; case study of, 116–18

beauty: brands, 130–31; as priority for moms, 133, 140–43, 147–50, 152. *See also* appeal and attractiveness; appearance

Beech Nut, 15

bicycles, bicycling, 45; safety and, 89, 90; tricycles and, 85

binge buying,134

Blackberry, 103

blacks, 160, 161

books, 62, 63, 114

Bravo, 136

breast-feeding, 13–14

budget: brands and, 127, 130; nutrition and, 14

bullies and bullying, 9, 113

busy-ness: of moms, 137–38; of moms of infants/toddlers, 14, 15, 129; of moms of middle schoolers, 24; of moms of preschoolers, 17, 133; of school-children, 7; technology and, 103, 106–7, 120; of teen lifestyle, 27

calendar: college, 73–74; family, 103

caregivers, communication with, 103, 105, 110, 113

case studies: of Barilla PLUS, 24, 25–26; of The Beatles Rock Band, 116–18, 124; of Educational Products Inc., 113, 114–15; of Frosted Flakes, 48; of iPhone, 105, 106–7; of Leap-Frog, 62, 63–64; of Luna, 4; of Mrs. Meyer's Clean Day, 84; of NikeiD, 50; of Purdue University, 73–74; research, 2–3, 169; of Rock Band, 117–18; of Sara Lee Soft & Smooth, 18, 19–20; of Skype, 121–22; of State Farm Insurance, 92, 93–94; of Suave (shampoo), 127, 129–31; of Target, 137–38; of Tonik, 97

cell phone use, 92; by children, 111–15, 149; by moms, 103–5, 109, 120, 124, 149; by teens, 116, 118–19; by young adults, 52. *See also* apps and applications; phone, phones

character development, 66, 74, 95. *See also* child development

chauffeurs, chauffeuring, 35, 46, 49. *See also* driver, drivers; driving

child development: of gross motor skills,14, 37–39; of infants and toddlers, 146–47; physical, 42–43; sports and, 53; television and, 65; toys and, 60–61

children: birth order of, 3, 8–9, 145, 162; communication of, with parents, 7–8; education

1, 135, 164; of religion, 136. *See also* influence of moms

influence of moms, 8, 31, 48; as bloggers, 105; on children, 20; on spending, 1, 4, 9, 146; on teens and young adults, 7, 27, 28, 29, 49, 68, 70, 95, 152, 157, 164–65

information sources: of moms, 65, 70, 80–81; teachers as, 113; websites as, 49, 88, 109

injury, injuries: bicycles and, 90; in elementary schoolchildren, 89; sports and, 36

instant messages, messaging (IM): 104, 113, 115, 116

insurance: automobile, 93; health, 80, 85, 95–96, 99. *See also under names of companies*

Internet: communication and, 103; homework and, 66; online research and, 80, 88; online safety and, 79; social media and, 9; use of, by moms, 104–10, 120. *See also* cyber safety and cyber threats; e-mail, e-mailing; instant messages, messaging; posts and posting

intersections: of brand and targeted moms, 152; of mindsets, 145, 154; of style and value, 143

interviews, 3; in-depth personal, 2; design of, 167–69; for jobs, 140, 142, 143; with management, about brands, 154; with moms, 14, 61, 70, 103, 104, 106, 115, 120, 121, 135, 156; qualitative, 13, 92, 159, 164, 167

iPhone: appeal of, 4, 105, 109, 124; case study of, 106–7; moms and, 103, 123; toddlers and, 61, 104, 146

iPod, moms and, 104, 110–11, 135

iTunes, 111

J.C. Penney, 133, 139

J. Jill, 134

JPMA (Juvenile Product Manufacturers Association), 81

Kohl's, 132, 133

leaders and leadership: brand, 1, 3, 29, 145, 152; sports and, 36, 47

LeapFrog: case study of, 63–64; education and, 74

learning: appeal of brands to, 63, 65, 67, 146; of children, as priority of moms, 41; outside classroom, 61, 69. *See also* education; school, schools

library, 1, 60; in school, 65

lifestyle, lifestyles; exercise and, 52; family, 27, 54, 148, 151; food and, 15, 20–21, 29; injuries related to, 89; outdoors, 86; sports and, 36, 41–45, 53, technology and, 105, 109, 120. *See also* healthy habits and lifestyle

literacy, 64

Luna: case study of, 40; Moms Club, 39, 53, 55, 151, 157

McDonald's, 16, 17, 18, 31

meals, 17, 20, 21, 23; brands and, 15, 25; breakfast, 16, 31; dinner,